Introduction

At the time of writing this book, I am forty-three years old and have been in the plumbing, heating, and gas trade for over twenty-three years. I have experienced good days . . . and bad. I try to embrace the thought that I still have years to go until I retire, but some days are harder than others when accepting that as the reality.

Writing this book has given me a chance to smile as I look back at the interesting people I have met, and the funny stories I have lived to tell. You have to have something to keep you going when the days get long and your patience runs short.

The funny thing is I never really aspired to become a plumber when I was a kid. I mean think about it. How many kids say to their parents, "When I grow up, I want to be a plumber"?

It just doesn't rank up there with being a fireman, lawyer, or doctor. But after trying a few different jobs in life, I wound up doing this . . . and you know what? I haven't really regretted it. This crazy trade has allowed me to have my own business, a cottage in the Cariboo region of British Columbia, a beautiful home, a beautiful wife, and has always put food on the table. That's not to say there haven't been many days when I swore it was my last day, but over the long run, I would recommend the trade to any young person looking for a good living.

This book is a collection of stories about all the interesting people I can remember over the years. I thought I would write it all down now because, to tell you the truth, I find my memory is not what it used to be. I can't count the number of times lately I go to my van to get a part, and stand there thinking, "What the hell did I come out here for?"

I hope you get a laugh out of this, as I did writing it. So grab a favorite beverage, sit down, and prepare to enter my world. It might make you appreciate your job a lot more, or wish you had become a plumber. I'm betting on the former, rather than the latter of the two choices.

Cheers.
Kevin

Sh*t Runs Downhill

A Collection of Stories and Life Lessons from a Plumber's Memoir

By

Kevin W. Batch

Strategic Book Publishing and Rights Co.

Strategic Book Publishing and Rights Co.
12620 FM 1960, Suite A4-507
Houston TX 77065
www.sbpra.com

ISBN: 978-1-61897-190-6

For my wife Wendy, without whom this book (and all else) would not have been accomplished. I love you with all my heart.

In Memory of Bob Fitchett.
During the editing of this book, our good friend from Wine Break passed away suddenly. His stories and laughter will be missed by many. Rest in peace, my friend.

Chapter 1

How Did I Wind Up with This Job?

For as long as I can remember, I have always liked to build things and work with my hands. My parents still attest to that, even to this day. I often remember me and my cousin, Murray, building stuff out of Lego blocks. He was always more creative than I was, but I didn't care. I always just enjoyed seeing a project, or in this case, a Lego building, come to life.

When I was a kid, I remember my dad going into the garage to build a dog house for a new puppy we had. I was very eager to help build this thing, so I proceeded to get my little work jeans on and go to the garage. I was pretty young, and thinking about it now, it was probably the wise choice for my dad to tell me I couldn't help him. A clumsy kid around circular saws is, maybe, not the best combination. I believe he said something about a "bull in a china shop," for whatever that's worth. I remember going inside crying, thinking I will never be as good as my dad at building or fixing stuff.

I also enjoyed any kind of puzzle I could get my hands on. I taught half my friends how to complete the Rubik's Cube. I guess that's where it all started. The combination of the two desires eventually put me into a job where I have to figure out the problem, then take something apart and attempt to fix it. This is the task of a service technician in the plumbing, heating, and gas trade. Unfortunately, it took quite some time for me to figure out my calling in life. Allow me to explain.

I always did fairly well in school, but never really focused on any one course. Writing this, I'm glad I took typing in grade eleven, although I must admit, I did it for the hot young ladies in the class. I always enjoyed woodwork, metalwork, and the trades. I still have some of the shitty stuff I built. Things like coffee tables, cutting boards, and plant holders.

I graduated high school with good marks, but rather than receiving praise for finally completing many years of school, the adults always asked the nagging question of, "So, what are you going to do now? College? Law school? University?" I didn't have a clue. I knew I wasn't lazy, but I had no idea what direction to go in.

I consulted with an old friend who was a few years older than me; a guy my parents thought was on the right track in life. (I bumped into this guy a few years ago. He weighs three hundred pounds at about five foot six and walks pretentiously with his mail-away bride. Mr. Know-it-all does not appear to be very successful today.) He suggested I get a Bachelor of Arts degree at a local college. My parents, of course, thought this was a grand idea. So, to please the powers that be, I signed up. To this day, I still don't know what the hell a Bachelor of Arts degree is, and that's probably the reason I lasted only a few weeks doing that. How does one get focused on taking courses, with no outcome or job status when they get out? It just didn't make sense to me.

At this point in life, I was enjoying myself and the freedom of no longer being in high school. I was hang'n out with my buddy Steve at the time. He lived just up the block from my parents' place, and we did everything together. Steve was really into computers and has a successful business of his own to this day. Computers just really weren't my thing. We couldn't wait to get jobs, so we could have our own money and independence. It also meant we could move out of Mom and Dad's place.

I recall my very first job was pumping gas at the local station. It was close enough that I could walk there, so I wasn't dependent on a car. I must admit, I had my license and couldn't wait for my first set of wheels. I knew this job wasn't going to last long, when I had the boss pull me in to have a "chat."

Why is it when a boss is about to give you shit in box car letters, they always seem to think it softens the blow when they start by asking remedial questions like, "So, how are you enjoying your time here?"

You say all the usual bullshit pleasantries in response, but really want to tell the truth. The truth being that you would rather shove toothpicks in your eyes than continue to work one more minute in this hell hole. Then comes the usual witty banter. I used to hate that.

I was told a customer came in with a diesel Volkswagen Rabbit. Apparently, I did not notice this, because I proceeded to fill his vehicle with regular gas. (I had wondered why the nozzle didn't seem to fit in the hole properly.) I figured the driver would notice right away with a mistake like that, as the car shouldn't even start. I guess it takes a bit of time for the fuel to get from the tank to the engine. Apparently, the family got quite far on their vacation road trip before the car "tapped out." My boss had to pay for their towing fee, the hotel for the night, and the cost to siphon the tank and get the proper fuel infused. Oops!

I soon quit that job (before they fired me) and started working at the local grocery store as a service clerk. They used to call us "service jerks" because we were the bottom of the food chain; pardon the pun. I ran to get price checks, did cleanups in whatever aisle, and always had to collect the shopping carts from the parking lot. What a job that was. The store was in a popular shopping mall, the equivalent of three square city blocks. People would quite often complete their shopping for groceries, and then decide to take their shopping cart with them all through the mall. I was the dumbass who had to retrieve them all at the end of the night. I'll bet I would retrieve over a hundred carts from all over that three-block parking lot in the course of an eight-hour shift. Thank God for being young and in shape, and having comfortable sneakers.

I was making good money for what I did. This was back in the days when the grocery industry was paying guys close to thirty dollars an hour to stock shelves. It was good money for an easy job with little to no formal education or training. Those wages no longer exist in that type of work now.

There were three owners of that store. One was a real smooth talker. Nothing seemed to bother him. He and I got along great. He had this really cool sports car he would bring to work. He would park it right in front of the store, get out, and toss me the keys.

"Hey, Kev. Find me a good spot in the shade."

The other two guys did not think of me in quite the same way. They would barely even talk to me. To this day, I don't know why. I thought I was a pretty nice kid. One day I went to hop over the chrome railing that held all the buggies together. As I did, the railing gave way and I got the support pole right in the spleen area, knocking the wind out of me. I soon had all the old ladies in the store trying to help me, and there's always that one guy who thinks he's a doctor. I was in a lot of pain, and it took a while to get my breath back. They eventually brought in some sort of medical staff to ensure I was alright. At the end of that day, one of the owners, who didn't like my kind, said to me, "Kid, you break one more thing in my store, and you're fired!"

I chose to quit before I asked him to step outside. I wasn't that big, but even if I only got a couple of shots in, I would be smiling. What an asshole!!

My dad worked in the automotive industry, so I thought maybe that was a good direction for me. He pulled a couple of strings and got me into a parts distribution warehouse. They specialized in auto, marine, and electric parts. I was asked if I had my driver's license. I did, and they promptly put me in as a driver to take parts orders to and from the various shops they had in the lower mainland.

I remember this little oriental guy named Brad showing me the routes. He was leaving soon to start computer school, so I was to be his replacement. It was the middle of February, and we just had a heavy snowfall a couple of days before. Certain areas of the roads were not plowed or salted as well as they should have been.

We had just been down to the Vancouver shop, where they proceeded to load my van with a huge pallet of brake shoe cores. These are quite heavy, and because we had other parts to deliver, they were not able to push the pallet far enough forward to balance the weight in the van. The problem was now the van had all the weight on the back tires, and nothing in the front. We began to head back to home base and proceeded down this big hill. Brad told me I would need to get into the right-hand lane, because the quickest way back would be to cut onto the freeway. As I changed lanes, I hit a large patch of slush. Because of little to no weight in the front, my tires were not able to gain traction. We were quickly picking up speed as the extra weight in the van was pushing us down the hill. The van lost control. I hit the brakes, but we just kept sliding. I still remember the sight and feeling as we slid uncontrollably downhill at about fifty miles an hour, heading straight for a wooden telephone pole. The last words I remember yelling were, "Hold on!"

The next thing I remember is Brad yelling at me to wake up. I guess the crash had knocked me unconscious for a few minutes. The van was propane powered, and I could smell the leaking fuel. The front windshield was completely shattered and pieces of it were in my lap. The van was propped up, and I remember wondering what we had landed on. It was the stumped remains of the shattered telephone pole we had hit. Brad kept telling me the van was going to blow! I felt like I was sitting beside Scotty from *Star Trek* when the engine room started to overheat and Kirk would ask him the status.

"She's about to blow!" he would say.

Lucky for me, a volunteer fireman had seen the whole thing happen and was yanking on the busted door trying to get me out. He succeeded in getting the door to open and told me he had shut the propane off. I was seeing everything double at this point, so knew I had done some cranial damage. As he attempted to get me out of the vehicle, we soon realized my lower left leg was pinned to the fuse panel. The pole had smashed the front end in so far the firewall had my leg pinned to the seat. They had to cut my pants and work boots to get me out.

I remember a huge crowd of people at this point, as I was walked to the ambulance. Traffic was backed up as far as the eye could see. Apparently, when I hit the pole, I caused the live overhead wires to come down on the road. No one could cross in either direction, as the wires were arcing and giving quite a light show. What a mess. But wait, it gets worse.

In an attempt to get the traffic moving, the volunteer firefighter decided to grab hold of the middle area of the overhead wires and pull on them to allow traffic to drive underneath them. (The police had not yet arrived.) This poor bastard was only trying to help, but it just wasn't his day. He succeeded in getting traffic to move, but once it did, an unsuspecting delivery truck came down the hill far too fast. He hit the same patch of slush I did, lost control, and hit the fireman head on.

I heard the ugly crack of body meeting grill, and that guy must have flown twenty feet in the air before he hit the ground. The paramedics who had been asking me if I was okay quickly ran to the aid of the fireman. It was obvious he had a broken arm and a couple of broken ribs.

They put both of us in the ambulance, and we made our way to the hospital. I remember him asking me what had happened. He seemed pretty out of it. I thanked him for pulling me out of the van and he responded with, "Who the hell are you?"

Upon arriving at the hospital, they wheeled us into separate rooms. I was now seeing normally and just wanted to wipe the blood from my face and go home. Apparently, when I hit the pole, my head smacked into the side window, along with the shattered glass. This was in the days before airbags. Because I was wearing a ball cap, it minimized the amount of abrasions on the upper area of my head.

A doctor came in and started poking and prodding me. "Does this hurt?" he kept saying. I remember him checking to see if my sternum was cracked. He pressed down on my chest bone. It hurt like hell. I held in the complete shrieking pain and said, "No, feels fine."

He pressed down again and asked if I was sure. I was sure of one thing: if he did it again, I was going to stick his stethoscope in an area that, I assume, it had never been in before. I repeated that I felt fine. He knew damn well it was hurting me, but decided against x-rays and released me. But first, I had to make a statement to the officer waiting outside the door. Yikes. I was sure they were going to charge me for something.

I had no idea what I had done or what law I had broken. Did they just need a statement or what? The officer asked how I was feeling and said my parents had been notified. My father was on his way to pick me up. He told me they interviewed three witnesses. One said I was speeding, the other two said I was not. There were no charges being laid. He looked me in the eye and said to me, "You're one lucky boy. You snapped that pole like a twig. It's a good thing it was old and rotten and not new or, even worse, a metal lamp pole. If so, we wouldn't be here talking right now. I've seen many accidents like this, and many don't make it. You might want to think about another line of work."

I had to chuckle as he said that and thanked him for his time.

My dad soon arrived to pick me up and, when I went into the hospital washroom to clean up, I didn't look all that bad for what I had just been through. I had a slight bump and cut on my left forehead, but my left shin could have used a couple of stitches. (I still have the scar to this day.) I was excited to tell my dad the big story, but he did not seem to think it was that big of a deal. In his mind, this was a fender bender, and I was exaggerating the story. That is, until we saw the wrecked van I had been driving.

We were stopped at a red light. I had just finished telling Dad the story, and when we crossed the intersection in front of us, there was this smashed van on a tow truck.

I think my dad's words were something along the lines of, "Holy shit." He then realized I was pretty lucky to walk away with just a few cuts and bruises on that one.

I took some time off to heal but went back to work the next week. They offered me a job putting orders together in the warehouse; anything to get me out of the trucks. My new nickname was "Crash," and there was a big, blown-up picture of my wrecked van from the paper in the lunch room. I enjoyed my brief working career there, but soon realized the automotive business was not for me.

The popular movie of the day was *Cocktail*, with Tom Cruise. I think every young kid who watched this movie wanted to be a bartender. So that's what my buddy Steve and I decided to do . . . we signed up for a bartending course.

Our parents forked out three hundred and fifty bucks, and the world was going to be our oyster, or so we thought. We both did well in the course and graduated with honors. We had far too much fun and drank too much, partying with the fellow students. But, back then, the late nights and hangovers were easily shaken off by the next morning.

During this course, Steve and I would often take off to the local nightclubs to study how the professionals did it. At least, that was our excuse. We would order the most complex shooters and drinks we could think of to test the bartenders. Looking back at this, we must have seemed like a couple of assholes. Anyway, one night we decided to go to a strip club. After a few cocktails, (a few too many), I decided making a move on one of the lovely ladies on the stage was a wise idea. Now, I know what you're thinking. "Kevin, you stupid bastard, they just want your tip money; you're wasting your time."

But, when you're confident, sometimes you accomplish things you never dreamt you could do. She met me for a drink after her show and gave me her number. We soon started dating.

So needless to say, I thought I was God's gift to the world. I had recently purchased my first car, a 1973 SS Nova, and it moved pretty good. Now I had some eye candy for a girlfriend, and I was going to be the next Tom Cruise of the bartending world—only much taller.

Steve and I just needed to find a job to bless the world with our newly acquired talents. Here's where reality smacks a young punk like myself square in the nuts. I must have gone to seven different interviews at restaurants or pubs that had ads in the papers. Each one of them asked what experience I had. Upon telling them I had none, but had graduated with honors from bartending school, they politely said, "Thanks for coming in. We'll give you a call."

Funny, that call never came. I realized at an early age sometimes you have to bullshit a little to get somewhere. So the next interview was at this shitty little pub out by some marina. I was desperate to get some work, as a girlfriend and fast car cost money. It came to the point in the interview when the manager asked me what experience I had.

At this point everything just kind of went into slow motion, and I had a vision of my favorite cartoon character, Bugs Bunny, saying to himself, "Think quick, rabbit."

If I didn't come up with a story, I was going to lose this job as well, so I looked him in the eye and confidently told him I worked at my cousin's bar in Alberta, Canada. It was called the Beef and Barrel. (The what? I chuckle now when I think of that bullshit made-up name!)

I was even cocky enough to say I had my cousin's number, if he needed to call for a reference. What the hell was I doing? If this guy called my bluff, I would have looked like a complete ass. But desperate times call for desperate measures, and he said, "No, that won't be necessary. When can you start?"

Thank God for shithouse luck. I started the next evening. My job title was a bar porter. I think the name "porter" must be ancient Greek for "he who gets all the shitty jobs." They had me cleaning tables, picking up empty beer mugs, and making sure the peanut and pretzel plates were always full. Did they not know of my supreme talents as a mixologist? That I was the next Tom Cruise of *Cocktail*?

Once again, reality gave me a swift kick in the 'nards as the bartender asked me to "tap the keg" for the Budweiser line. Wait a minute. They didn't teach us this in bartending school. I knew in theory what she wanted me to do. I just didn't know how. Once again, ol' Bugs was in my thoughts, saying, "Think quick, rabbit," and I proceeded to go into the back cooler and attempt to complete this daunting task.

I tried to figure this one out on my own with common sense; this is a pressurized vessel. If I don't do this right, I'm going to have a complete mess of beer spraying everywhere, not to mention all over me, and I had my best shirt on!

After trying for a few minutes to figure it out, I pulled my bartender aside and told her the truth. She asked what experience I had, and I admitted to her that I bullshitted my way through the interview to get the job.

Upon asking her to show me how to tap the keg and to please not rat me out to the boss, she just gave me that disapproving head shake. You know the one; the one when you tell your parents you want to be a ventriloquist or a magician. That evening the boss pulled me aside, and I was told not to come in for my shift tomorrow. My final, and only, check would be mailed to me.

On the drive home that night, I thought many things. How do I tell my parents? How do I tell my buddy Steve? What do I tell my girlfriend? I had quit jobs, but it's a different feeling being fired. What do I do now for work?

Looking back at it now, I laugh and thank the good Lord the job didn't work out. Maybe I was meant for better things. I now know what they mean when they say Hollywood can make anything look glamorous. I would not have been able to put up with the pressure on busy nights, the shitty hours, and dealing with drunks. Ah well, I never really wanted to be Tom Cruise anyway.

Chapter 2

"Mom, Dad? I'm Dating a Stripper."

I was still dating this young lady and the crazy thing is I hadn't quite summoned the nerve to tell my parents. Are you kidding me? My parents were old school and, if I told them what she did for a living, I think they would have disowned me. Turns out, they almost did, but we'll get to that. They knew I was dating someone, but couldn't figure out why I hadn't introduced her and why I was always meeting her very late at night. She would end her shows around two in the morning, and I would meet her for a drink, then head back to her place. She was living in the basement of her folks' place.

I got to know her parents quite well and I have to say, they were two of the greatest people I have had the privilege to know. At this point, I was actually starting to show some maturity as the whole thrill of dating an exotic dancer had kind of faded, and I was now looking at getting her out of that crazy shit and into a real job with a future. Believe me, it was also what her parents had wanted for quite some time.

I remember her dad sitting me down one night over a few too many adult beverages. I received the speech. You know the one, the one that starts with, "So, are you thinking of shacking up with my daughter?"

He was a great guy who genuinely cared for my well being and my future. He stated that, if I was going to marry his daughter one day, I had to have a good job. He then made me an offer I couldn't refuse.

Her dad was pretty high up in the company he worked for and had some pretty good pull. He asked if I had ever tried my hand at drafting. I had done a bit in high school and rather liked it. Come to think of it, I wasn't bad at it either. He knew of a teacher/friend of his that taught at a local college. It was a year of schooling, full time, and if I passed the course, he would get me a job at the firm where he worked. Wow! A suit and tie job. That will show the world I'm somebody! That will make my parents proud!

Looking back, I don't think I ever stopped to ponder if this was something that would make ME proud of me.

We gave each other a gentleman's handshake that suggested we would both be good on our word. At this point, I had to tell my parents who I was dating and what my newfound path of life would be, the latter being the easy part.

I remember going upstairs to ask for a family discussion. My parents sat looking at me with disdain and a general mood of apprehension. I began by breaking the ice with some kind of rhetoric babble, but when telling them about the new love of my life, my mother stood up and blurted out, "She's a HOOKER, isn't she!"

It was all I could do to contain my laughter while still trying to stay serious. "What? Are you nuts?" I said. "No, she's not a hooker; what the hell would make you think that?"

I guess picking her up at the clubs late at night had led them to believe the worst . . . but a hooker? I looked at my dad for some kind of rational thinking, but he looked just as befuddled as my mom.

After explaining to them what she did for a living, they didn't take the news much easier. I assured them it was only temporary until she could find some other sort of employment, or until she could enroll in some further education. I have to say, my life was easier when I was living the lie and not telling them. After this news, it was a constant bicker session at my place, so I eventually decided to move out and live with my girlfriend in her parent's basement suite. Listen closely, kids; there's a lesson here to be learned.

I should have gone the mature route and sat down for another family discussion, but I knew how that was going to turn out. I also should have eased into breaking the news to my parents, but that was just not my style at the time. I waited until they were going out for a Sunday drive, packed up all my shit, and moved it to my new digs at my girlfriend's place. Wow! That decision did not go over well.

When my parents got home to find me gone, my dad somehow got their number and phoned the house. He had it out with her dad and then with me. I guess they didn't realize no one had pushed me; this was done entirely of my own free will.

My mother, especially, has always had a hard time letting her only child spread his wings to make his own mistakes. I understand it now, but at the time it was always a struggle. My dad ended up writing me a heartfelt note about how disappointed he was in me, but, should I ever need to come back home, I was always welcome. Of course, not without an apology and the acceptance of the "My house, my rules" regime.

For the sake of this story, we'll call our exotic dancer Lola. Needless to say, I was quite smitten with this girl. She was a bit of a tomboy who knew more about cars than I did. She liked sports and knew how to party. Not to mention, she had one hell of body. But after the great sex gets routine, you have to have something else in common. I'm not sure we did. Looking back, we were both a couple of kids just trying to find our path in life. The strange thing was, as our relationship started to fade, my relationship with her parents began to grow.

I grew very fond of her mom, who was one hell of a cook. They were English, and every Sunday was roast dinner with Yorkshire pudding and gravy. Awesome! Her dad was a real man's man. He loved to put back a few pints, play golf, and work around the yard on the weekend. I learned a lot from him. It became a strange dynamic when I felt I needed to break it off with Lola, but I did not want to leave the comforts and relationship I had with her parents. I felt independent as well. They really made me feel part of the family.

Eventually, Lola and I decided to move out on our own. We had a nice little basement suite not far from her folks. Unfortunately, it was also close to an ex-boyfriend's place. I eventually found out he was coming over to "visit" while I was at work, if you know what I mean. I eventually caught on and decided enough was enough. I broke up with Lola but decided I still wanted to go ahead with drafting school. My motivation was no longer about marrying her but having a real trade behind me.

I moved back to my parents' place to start over and get back to my roots.

My dad and I eventually patched things up, and he paid for the drafting course I was about to begin. He drove me in the morning on his way downtown to work. I took the bus home.

I'm not sure if my mother has ever forgiven me to this day for moving out unannounced; it's not a subject I bring up often around her. I needed to find my independence; I hope she's able to see that now. Unfortunately, I didn't go about it with any form of grace or maturity, just with the bullheaded stubbornness of a young buck.

I finished the course and, true to his word, Lola's dad got me a job at the engineering firm where he worked. I needed reliable transportation to my new job, so Dad and I decided we would go shopping for a car together. This is when you really get to experience something called the generation gap.

Up to this point, I had been surviving on my muscle cars that looked cool but constantly broke down. He somehow convinced me to purchase a Mazda 626. This is, without a doubt, the nerdiest car on the face of the planet. Going from a '73 SS Nova to a Mazda 626 is like going from partying with Charlie Sheen to partying with Mr. Rogers. But, with the amount of headaches I had caused my dad over the last year, I decided to just go with his wisdom and get the reliable car. I had to get my head around the fact I was now going to be an "adult" with a real job in a real downtown office.

Life was changing rather quickly for me. After purchasing an assortment of suits, ties, and cologne, I was ready to start my new job. I'll never forget my first day. Keep in mind that, at this point, I'm still into loud rock music and my hair was a little on the long side.

I walked into this stuffy office building with a bunch of stuffy engineers who all thought their shit smelled like roses. Just a mass of suits with perfect short haircuts and a ton of Brylcream. I did not own a pair of dress shoes and also thought I should look a little more "hip," so I wore my cowboy boots with my slacks. I will now admit it was not a great look, but at the time I thought I was looking good. The truth is I stood out like a sore thumb.

I went to take the elevator to the next floor of the office when a smug young engineer walked in with me. I tried to be polite by saying, "Hello, I'm Kevin, the new guy." He just looked me up and down and said, "Nice shoes; where's your horse?"

Honestly, I didn't know whether to laugh, say excuse me, or knock his fucking lights out for being a smart ass. This guy probably weighed a hundred and sixty-five pounds, and was all of five foot six. Looking back, I should have asked him if they had a good dental plan here, then proceeded to help him pick up his teeth as I hit him with a right cross. Not a good way to start your first day, but it would have been good talk around the water cooler.

I had just assumed they would put me in some sort of designing or drafting that I knew something about. Like houses or drawings on how to put shit together. (To this day, I get frustrated with IKEA instructions.) No, that would just be too easy. They put me in something called Materials Handling.

I had never heard of this in my entire time at the drafting course. Hell, I had never heard of this in my entire life. I quickly found out it is the designing of conveyor belts, hoppers, crushers, and rollers. These designs are mainly used in the mining industry.

Large machines dug the rock from open pit mines, and it was our job to design the system that broke the rock down to small sizes and then transferred it to different areas of the site via conveyor belts.

What the hell was I doing in this department? It was like putting Tiger Woods in a monogamous relationship. I did not know anything about it and was completely out of my element.

But now what? My parents had paid good money for this course, not to mention my time and effort of a whole year in school. I couldn't tell them, or Lola's dad, I was not familiar with this area of drafting and would not accept the position. I was prepared to tough it out and make the best of it, hoping it would get better.

I slowly got to know a few chosen people and tried to fit in. It was not easy. Most of these people had personalities as dull as a butter knife, and they were fat, donut-eating smokers who wouldn't know anything about sports, let alone have ever played one. Not the type of people I respected. Don't get me wrong; they were very intelligent at what they did, but just drones behind a draft board or computer.

But there was a side to this I hadn't realized. The single ladies of the office had not seen someone of my type and began to take notice. I've never been mistaken for Brad Pitt in the looks department, but I've always kept in good shape and have been told on occasion I'm not hard to look at. So this became my motivation for going to work at this mundane shit hole.

I remember chatting up one of the ladies in accounting. Her name was Naomi and she had a body that would not quit. I vaguely remember taking her to dinner and then a comedy club. I got rather drunk after that and remember taking her back to her place, only to find out she was still living with her ex-boyfriend. Needless to say, not a lot happened for my sex life that night.

I was eventually put on another project and our bookkeeper was a blast. She wasn't the cutest thing I had ever seen, but she often wore low-cut tops and had a lovely rack, if you know what

I mean. She loved to party, drink, and laugh. I'm thinking this is my kind of gal! Her name was Vicki and we became good party buddies. We decided to go out for a drink one night. Only problem was, it was a Wednesday night and we didn't stop at one drink. We partied the night away and ended back at her place around three in the morning. I tried to make a move, but who was I kidding? I was too drunk to do much of anything. It would have been like playing pool with a rope. I remember her saying something to the likes of, "You wouldn't be able to handle me anyway."

I kind of think she was into some crazy, kinky stuff. Anyway, I crashed on the couch and we both somehow made it to work the next day. I'm pretty sure I was still drunk until about lunch time. We ended up signing up for the company softball team and had many a good night of drinking a laughing. We never slept together; we just had a good time hangin' out.

Looking back, maybe that was best. Maybe, she was too much for me to handle. She was probably right; I was still a pretty naïve kid and would have probably been traumatized for life with nightmares of her probable kinky escapades.

At this point, I was beginning to get a bit of a reputation. My partying ways had reached the higher ups, and I was eventually hauled in to the chief's office. He was an old school Scotsman, and you could tell he kind of liked me, but he had a firm to run and had to lay down the law.

He proceeded to tell me my work was slipping, and he wanted me to take these night courses to improve my knowledge of the designs and engineering. I agreed, reluctantly, and proceeded to go to two night classes a week at the British Columbia Institute of Technology. It's the big trade school in Western Canada, and anyone who wants to have a good education in trades usually graduates from there.

I was bored to tears and just did not have the heart to continue this charade any longer. Not bored because I knew the mathematics and logarithms inside and out, bored because

I didn't have a clue what I needed to learn this shit for anyway. This became one of the most frustrating times of my life. I was stuck in a job where I never was able to see the final product I was drafting. I was not able to use my hands to build anything. This was not the job for me, and I could not look in the mirror for the rest of my working days knowing I had to do this until retirement. There had to be a better way.

The interesting thing is, the next day of work, I stopped to just enjoy the view of downtown Vancouver. I remember looking out of my office window at a construction worker. It was the middle of winter, and this poor bastard was working on a tower across the street. At this point, the tower was only concrete floors and pillars. The rain was almost turning to snow and it was blowing at an angle, so even the concrete platform above him was not keeping him dry. I'm not sure if he was a plumber or electrician, but he looked cold, and I shook my head thinking, *Man, am I glad I'm not doing that for a living.* Little did I know what was in my future.

It was not long after this I was asked to sit down with my boss, the old Scotsman. He asked me how the night classes were going, and something inside me just kind of snapped. I didn't get angry or hostile; I just kind of went into this pleading realm of honesty. That's about the only way I can describe it.

I began to tell him the honest truth. I explained I was not cut out for these courses, nor did I want to continue to show up for them. When he proceeded to tell me I had to complete these courses to hold my job, I remember telling him maybe I was not cut out to do this job either. Upon leaving his office, a cold chill came over me as I thought to myself, "Holy shit, did I just tell my boss I was not cut out for my job?" It was almost surreal, like an out of body experience. I couldn't believe what I had said, but it somehow instilled a quiet comfort that took a weight off my shoulders.

Not surprisingly, a couple of weeks later, I received my layoff notice. I was obviously heartbroken and had a million thoughts run through my head. What do I do now? How do I break this to my parents? How do I face my ex's dad, who stuck his neck out to get me the job? How do I hold my head up in front of these stuffy engineers, as they look at me like a lower class citizen who couldn't hold a job with the big boys? I was still a kid trying to make a go of it in this adult world. It had felt like I failed.

I expected very little in the way of good-bye and good luck, but I was surprised at how many people walked up to me and wished me all the best. One of the guys I had become friends with was from the Czech Republic. He had recently moved to Canada, and this was his first big job. He had a wife and kid to support. His name was Miklos. He was laid off the same day I was. He shook my hand and assured me both he and I would be just fine. We would land on our feet. It was great to hear him say that, every day, I had made him laugh. I can only hope he did land on his feet. Other people I thought didn't give a shit if I lived or died came over to say good-bye and wish me well. I was pleasantly surprised at the heartfelt wishes of good luck for the future.

But I'll always remember the old Scotsman, my boss, Bill. As he gave me my walking papers, he said something I have never forgotten. He said to me, in his thick Scottish accent, "You know, Kevin, I've noticed in life sometimes people are meant for different things. If this isn't where your heart is, then go find your passion. I think maybe you were meant for something better than this. I wish you well in finding it, son."

He was a wise man, that old Scotsman, and I know today what he was trying to tell me.

Chapter 3

What Do I Need to Know to be a Plumber?

I always laugh when the average Joe says plumbing is easy. You always get the run of the mill comments that you only need to know three things to be a plumber: shit runs downhill, payday's on Friday, and don't stick your fingers in your mouth. This is usually told by the drunkest guy at the party. When I'm sure I have everyone's attention for my rebuttal, I look them right in the eye and calmly say, "And every asshole's a potential customer!"

It usually takes the crowd, and the drunken guy, a few seconds to decipher I just underhandedly called this jerk an asshole. It's one of my favorites and I have used it many times. There is a reason why we go to school for four years: it's not as easy as people think. Sure, you can go to your local Home Depot and talk to the plumbing guy in aisle seven. He's going to make it sound real easy. That's when Joe Homeowner gets the impression, just because he fixed a leak on his kitchen tap, he's now a plumber. I love that kind of guy, because he's the one who tries to fix his neighbors' plumbing problems a couple of weeks later and ends up fucking it up completely. I get the phone call from the wife to come fix it on the Monday morning when he's gone to work, and it quite often takes me twice as long to fix the extra screw-ups he made. But I digress.

Back to our story.

I was laid off from my drafting fiasco . . . er . . . job, and was now making phone calls to other drafting firms, but work was slow all over. It was the late eighties and our economy was at a bit of a low point, if I recall correctly. I felt a little better knowing summer was almost upon us, and if you had to pick a time to get laid off, well, this was as good a time as any.

One would also think living at Mom and Dad's meant I would be saving money on rent, and there was no pressure at all, right? Wrong. You see, my parents, as I mentioned before, were old school. God forbid I am not part of the gainfully employed group of society. That wouldn't be prudent, not at this juncture.

I recall a couple of days after the layoff looking outside my basement window to see a beautiful, sunny day. I did what any good Canadian kid would do. I grabbed the most comfortable lawn chair I could find, put a cold six-pack in a bucket of ice, and brought out a radio to enjoy the sunshine. I was contemplating what I was going to do with my summer off and my unemployment insurance money. Ah, the endless possibilities.

Well, that was quickly squashed when my mother proceeded to come out on the balcony and give me the speech on how I better get my act together. If I thought I was going to drink beer and party the summer away . . . I had another thing coming. Parents can be such a downer.

The bickering began to be a bit much when my dad soon followed suit. I'd had enough of this bullshit and decided to figure out how I was going to, once again, move out. I had started to hang out with an old school friend, Rob. He was a cool character, really easygoing, and had a great, nonchalant attitude about life. We started mountain biking and hitting the gym together. We soon started hitting the clubs and making the moves on the ladies. Not to sound gay—not that there's anything wrong with that—but Rob was a good-looking guy. The ladies flocked to him and, with me being his new wingman, I was starting to meet a lot more women.

We decided to move out and get a basement suite together where it would be, as we called it, SHAG-RE-LA! I don't know how I thought I was going to afford it, but I knew something would come up. Besides, Rob was still in college and he wasn't worried about how he was going to afford it. I figured that was the key; stop worrying so much about money and just go with the flow.

I remember looking for a suite. I found this place not too far from his and my parents. This is, of course, always a wise decision, because you are close enough to do extra laundry and go over for Sunday dinner. I remember meeting the landlord and his wife. He was from Croatia, and his wife was a local girl who had gone to the same high school as me and Rob back in the day.

I could not help but notice she was rather large in the belly area, but tried not to stare. As we talked about school and old teachers, she started talking about her baby. I was desperate to try and get on her good side because I really liked the suite. I quickly said, "Oh, the baby. How nice. When are you due?"

She had that awkward look on her face as she looked at me and said, "I had her two months ago; we named her Ella."

Oops. There is an example of not thinking before you talk. I quickly changed the subject, as I must have gone a few shades of red. I felt like an asshole.

Somehow, we got the suite—no thanks to my witty banter—and life with Rob was great, for a while. I slowly realized this guy was the biggest slob I had ever lived with.

I remember having to get a phone number from his room. I had trouble opening the door because his dirty laundry was piled over a foot high. I'm not exaggerating! I would come home after a good weekend at a lady friend's place, only to find an actual mountain of cigarette butts in the ashtray, moldy remnants of some Kraft dinner in a pot on the stove, and him sleeping in his underwear on the couch, snoring away.

"Oh . . . hey dude. I was going to clean up, but I didn't think you'd be home until later."

Rob was an awesome guy, but I knew this was not going to last long.

I finally started warming up to the idea that continuing my career as a draftsman was not the path I would take for my life.

But now what? I was getting restless and knew I had to find some kind of work. I was chatting with an old acquaintance one day about my situation when he told me a mutual friend needed some help on a job site. His name was John, and he and his dad ran a plumbing company.

I had known John since kindergarten, and also knew his dad, as he had been a soccer coach and a Cub Scout master alongside my dad when I was a kid. We used to be pretty close back in the elementary school days. We often did homework or class projects together. We also shared a fondness for our favorite band of the day, Kiss!—I still pull their albums out now and then. In fact, thinking about it now, I remember we made costumes and went as Kiss one year for Halloween. I was Ace Frehley.

I remember calling John and catching up on old times. After a few laughs, I told him of my current situation with my job, or lack thereof. Their company was currently putting the plumbing in at a new apartment condo being built, in Chilliwack! Just to put that into a distance perspective, this would be close to a two-hour drive from where I lived, a long drive at best. He asked if I was interested in giving them a hand.

I thought about it and came to the conclusion I had nothing to lose. Gas was at a somewhat reasonable price back in '89, so I really didn't worry about the travel. After all, I had my nerdy Mazda 626, good on gas and reliable, just like my dad had promised. I would also get a chance to hang out with my old buddy, John, and surely have some laughs. But what would I be doing and what did I need to know to be a plumber?

He told me to be at the job site by seven thirty in the morning. Holy shit. Seven thirty! That would mean I would have to be up and out the door by five thirty. This would be a shock to the system, as I had become quite used to sleeping in. I would often get up at the crack of noon.

I have never been a morning person. I hate getting up early to this day, but I dragged my ass out of bed and into the shower. I grabbed a cup of java for the trip and off I went.

I remember seeing the sun rise over the mountains. I couldn't remember the last time I had seen that; it was beautiful. I made it on time and immediately felt out of place, as I parked my nerdy little white Mazda amongst all the huge pickup trucks.

I was wearing running shoes with jeans and a Windbreaker. All the other construction guys were in steel toed boots with jean jackets or mackinaws. Once again I felt out of place on the first day of the job.

I definitely had some stares and second looks, as I can only imagine what these guys must have thought of me. I asked one guy if he knew where the plumbers hang out. He took the cigarette out of his mouth just long enough to hack, spit, and simply point to the underground parking garage. I walked down to eventually find John and the crew. After exchanging the regular pleasantries, he introduced me to the guys.

There was Jim, a journeyman plumber around his late thirties. Nice guy, kind of kept to himself. There was Jerry. He and I took to each other right away, as he was a crazy bastard, probably in his late forties. He immediately took me under his wing and was eager to answer any questions I had.

And then there was Fred. Ah, yes . . . Fred! This guy was an interesting study. He was a second-year apprentice in the trade at this time, but had to be in his early forties. This would be a little late to get in the trade, one would think, but he had an interesting story.

Upon first introduction to this guy, he was very soft spoken and somewhat shy—almost socially inept, one could say. He was a pretty solid guy, built like a brick shithouse, standing at six feet, maybe two hundred and thirty pounds. He seemed mild mannered, but I wouldn't want to get on his bad side. Sure enough, I eventually did, but we will get to that.

He was from the area we were working in, Chilliwack. This area is known for being the Bible belt of the Fraser Valley and Greater Vancouver area, and he was most certainly religious.

I remember shaking his hand thinking, *Wow, this guy could crush a tennis ball with minimal effort.* I chatted with him to find out he had been in the logging industry prior to this. He was a faller, and judging by the size of the guy, probably a pretty good one. Apparently, he was the victim of a serious accident when a thick tree came back on a bad angle and smashed him across the neck and back. I believe he was hospitalized for quite some time with broken neck vertebrae and a couple of cracked ribs. He lived to tell the tale and to once again see his wife and children.

I assume it was at this point he became religious and decided to pick a new career; can't say I blame him. He and I were destined to clash because I'm sure he looked at me as a sinner and did not approve of my partying ways. I later began to see he was jealous of my long-time friendship with John. I began to become a threat to his moving up the company ladder, as I would often get the jobs he thought he deserved and was more qualified to do.

I was quickly fitted for a hard hat and given my first job in my plumbing career: carrying toilets up three flights of stairs . . . all day! I guess we all have to start somewhere.

The building was a wood frame building without an elevator, commonly known as a "walk up." I had to take the toilets to each of the individual suites. Then it was bringing the two- and three-inch cast iron pipe to whatever floor the guys were working on.

I quickly learned that a three inch diameter by ten foot long piece of cast iron pipe weighs much more than it looks.

There is a proper way to carry it that makes it quite easy, though. By balancing the middle of the pipe on the meaty part of your shoulder, you can carry large amounts of weighted pipe. They actually teach you this in first year plumbing school.

I remember thinking this wasn't what I'd figured I'd be doing. But I did realize one thing quickly: wow, was I out of shape! By the end of that day, I couldn't wait to get home and crack a cold beer. I was wiped!

I did this for pretty much a week. My feet were killing me, as I had to purchase a pair of steel toed boots and, as any construction guy will tell you, they are not very comfortable. They are even less comfortable when you purchase a cheap pair, like I did. Let that be a lesson to you, kids. Spend money on good footwear; it's worth it! I had blisters on my blisters, but was starting to get calluses on my hands. Could this be the slow transformation from wimpy suit and tie office clown to manly construction guy? I felt like mild mannered Clark Kent going into the phone booth to become Superman!! I began to fit in.

The first thing I noticed was construction guys swear, a lot! There is constant cursing and every sentence has at least one, sometimes two, F-bombs inserted for your pleasure. Smoking heavily is also an asset to fitting in. Not one that I would recommend, but it did seem to be part of the scene.

My wardrobe began to change as well. My dress shirts and ties soon moved to the back of the closet, as I needed more room for my thermal shirts, heavy denims, and mackinaw jackets. It was also easier in the mornings.

When I worked at the office downtown, I would have to ensure I was well groomed, shaved with gel in the hair and a bit of cologne. Now, it was shaving-optional, no cologne, and a ball cap was fine because, for most of the day, you're in a hardhat anyway. You're grubby and sweaty when you get home, so it makes more sense to shower then.

I remember John pulling me aside one Friday after work. We would always have a cold case of beer ready for the end of the week. I guess I had been there about a month at this point, and I was asked if I liked it. The commute was kind of tough, but other than that, I really felt like this is what I was meant to do. I really enjoyed the fact you had a part in a project coming to life. To see the transformation of a bunch of wood, concrete, and dirt turning into a working building was a great feeling. In drafting, you would design or draw the details of how to build something, but never get to build it. You would never get to see the final product. Now, I was on the other side of the fence, and it just felt right. Even the other tradesmen on the job site were a breath of fresh air. Most of these guys were down-to-earth people, honest and hard working. Typical average Joes who are just trying to feed their families and make ends meet. Not pretentious or stuck up, like some I had met at my last job.

John asked me if I wanted to make it into a permanent position and be on the crew full time. I went home that weekend and really had to think about what I wanted to do. How would my parents feel after all the time and money put into drafting school, college, and bartending school? All of which I was, now, going to just walk away from.

My dad was pretty supportive and said he noticed I wasn't really happy doing the drafting thing. He was also impressed I was getting up every morning to drive to Chilliwack to do this. I had his blessing. At that point, I went back Monday morning to tell John I wanted full time employment.

I began to do some real plumbing as opposed to just being the grunt of the job site. I was putting cast iron piping together for the soil and vent stacks. Soldering was something I was introduced to and was good at it from the moment I tried it.

My mom says when I was a kid I used to love to play with matches. Good thing I got into plumbing instead of pyromania. There is definitely an art to soldering a good joint. The key is not to overheat the fitting, or to use too much solder. A good tradesman should only need a half inch of solder for a half inch pipe fitting, a three-quarter inch length of soldier for a three-quarter inch pipe fitting, and so on.

I remember soldering up bath/shower diverters for all the tubs in the buildings. After ten or so, John came down to see how shabby my work would be and how many leaks I would have. To his surprise, there were zero leaks and nice clean joints. To this day, I can't stand to see plumbers' joints with a ton of solder dripping down the pipe and all over the fitting. It's messy and there's no excuse for it. Take some pride in your work.

I was starting to gain John's confidence and wanted to take on more responsibility. He started to give me some, and I loved it.

Working with my hands and being able to see what I have done, I had finally found my passion.

Now, let me explain something. It's not like I would wake up every morning jumping out of bed doing cartwheels with excitement to go to work. I think we can all agree anything you have to do eight hours a day, five days a week is eventually going to get a little monotonous and drawn out. But it's a better feeling than waking up counting the days until you can retire, get laid off, or get fired. You might as well be serving a prison sentence. Life's too short to have to wake up every day feeling like that. Thank the good Lord for things having a way of working themselves out.

If you're reading this and feeling this way about your job, I challenge you to look up the effects on the body that stress causes. Life is a lot easier to face every day when you're not looking down the barrel of the gun most people call a job; in reality, it's a cancer that takes a little more of your soul away each day. The company eventually indentured me with the government plumbing program, which means you get signed up to start your journey of becoming a full-fledged tradesman, commonly known as a journeyman.

I'm not sure if it's still done this way today, but years ago the plumbing trade was four separate years of schooling. Each year is six weeks of classroom time, five days a week, eight hours a day. Your final year was eight weeks, with the option of taking your gas ticket as well.

Once you had the required amount of hours on the actual job site, and passed all the exams, you were given a journeyman status that allows you to be recognized in any province in Canada. You can also challenge the government exam. If you pass it, you receive what is known as a T.Q. or tradesman qualification that is only good in British Columbia.

There were some ups and downs working with/for an old friend. It's often said that one should never mix business and friendship. I now understand how true that is. Allow me to explain.

Chapter 4

Life with John

Allow me to give you a quick background on John. He's the type of guy who is just a born leader. He was the guy who would start the trend, never the guy to follow it. The type of guy who was good at anything he put his mind to, and he was always doing something. He had this huge multicar garage/workshop at his folks' place. He was notorious for taking cars apart, rebuilding them or improving their power, and then putting them back together. He could weld, do body work, interior work, or put an engine together. The crazy thing is he would often do this after work until maybe midnight. Then he'd be up at six in the morning to start his day. Most would call him an overachiever.

I always looked up to him and wanted to have his talent. He was always the guy I looked to for help in elementary and high school, when I couldn't figure out a question or assignment. He would always encourage me to figure it out myself, but would always give me a hand if I couldn't. I'm sure we all know a guy like that, the guy who has a million tools and can do anything. Most times, guys like that are braggers and real pain in the ass know-it-alls. But John was different. He was loyal to his friends and a very humble guy. If there was one guy in life I wanted to emulate, it was him.

Looking back, I was probably a victim of kissing his ass and trying everything to be his "best friend." But the problem was he had tons of friends who felt the same way I did. He always had guys asking him for favors. Guys would come over on a weeknight and get John to fix their car. When they would say,

"Thanks, what do I owe you?" John would just say, "Nothing, just buy me a beer some time." He was just that sort of guy. He had a very tight-knit group of friends, and it was hard to break into this cliquey group.

As we were now well into the condo project, the first half of the building was complete. Not all the suites were purchased, so there were a few vacant ones available. The selling prices included all new appliances. John had become somewhat of a friend to the owner, who was also the site general foreman. He convinced the guy to let us stay in one of the empty apartments from Monday through Friday of the work week. This was great; I would no longer have to travel back and forth to Burnaby every day. I still had Rob as a roommate back home, so he took care of things while I was away. There were fast-food joints all around the area, a cold beer and wine store, and, most importantly, a nightclub a few blocks away.

At this time, John had hired a couple of his buddies to be the grunts, or helping hands, on the job site. Since I was moving up the ladder, he needed some help bringing the fixtures up the stairs and/or going to the plumbing wholesalers to get parts. He brought in a friend named Doug, and a guy he knew from the Cariboo area of British Columbia named Brad. These two guys were as backwoods as they come, country boys with the chewing tobacco in their teeth to prove it. I had met and hung out with Doug a few times, but didn't know Brad all that well. We got to know each other rather quickly, because the four of us were now living in a two-bedroom condo with one bathroom. It would turn out to be the start of a real gong show.

I had an old sponge mattress I used to use when I would go camping. I used that under my sleeping bag and had the living room as my bedroom area. I don't remember if we drew straws, but somehow I got screwed out of having the comfy, quiet bedroom. We were all in our early twenties, and we all loved to party, maybe a little too much. Brad and Doug could really put the beers back. John was a pretty wiry guy who didn't weigh that much. He could put the beers back, but liked to drink whiskey and bourbon. Let's just say he liked the whiskey, but the whiskey did not like him. He would turn into a bit of an asshole when he drank that shit. It also made him afraid of nothing. I've seen that guy ride a snowmobile in the middle of summer around a lake. No shit! His parents have an old cabin on the shore of Eagan Lake in the British Columbia Interior. One sunny afternoon, he revs up the snowmobile and proceeds to take a hundred-foot run at top speed down the dirt- and rock-filled boat launch area. He was able to gather enough speed to hit the water and plane on top of it. He drove that snowmobile from one side of the lake to the other and back. Unbelievable! If he had bet me twenty bucks it could be done, I would have said no way. But that was John.

We would finish work at around four thirty. One of us would head to the beer and wine store for some cold pops, and we would generally order a pizza for dinner. It was now the middle of summer, and we were situated on the top floor of a three-floor condo. As I had mentioned most, but not all, of the suites had been bought. We were close to the Chilliwack hospital and, every now and then, I would see this beautiful nurse come home from her shift. I would flash her a smile and say hello, but she mostly kept to herself. I noticed she did not have a wedding ring on, and that she lived somewhere in the complex. There were only about fifteen units rented at this time, so if I kept my eyes open I was sure I would be able to figure out what area of the building she resided in. I eventually did . . . and then some!

I would quite often sit out on our small balcony to enjoy the fresh air of the Fraser Valley and get some sun, but also to get some privacy and quiet time from the three amigos. Being on the top floor of the building, we had a pretty good view of the surrounding area and the rest of the suites. It was just past twilight, and I noticed my favorite little intern coming home from a long day at work. She obviously did not notice me, as I was perched high above on the third-floor balcony. I felt like an eagle watching for his prey, except I was an eagle with a cold beer in one hand and a piece of pizza in the other.

It was nearly dark when I noticed a light go on in a suite down on the first floor. It appeared to be a bedroom area, as I would decipher, noticing the bed and dresser with a big mirror on top. The occupant had the blinds down for privacy, but they were turned at such an angle that I looked directly through the slots and into the room. I noticed this beautiful lady staring at herself in the bedroom dresser mirror. It was the same nurse I had been admiring for the last few weeks. I proceeded to watch as the clothes came off, one by one. Hmm . . . Dear Penthouse . . . She slowly entered the shower and, in my head, I could hear the bad seventies porno music begin to play. You know the type, bow chicka wow wow . . . chicka wow wow. Either that or the slow baritone notes of Barry White, whatever gets you in the mood.

It was the weirdest thing. In one way, you feel rather guilty and sheepish, but on the other hand, you think, *What are the chances of this happening?* It's like a train wreck; you don't want to look, but you can't take your eyes off of it. Then, of course, my young, over-horny mind starts to wander. I told myself, *ya, she knew I was out here lookin' at her and purposely turned the blinds this way. Pretty soon she'll be seeing me in the parking lot and winking at me, asking if I've been a bad boy!*

Then I realized that was the beer doing the thinking. But, I did put the thought process together that if she went into the shower naked, she would have to come out of the shower . . . naked! Yes, I was pretty astute at that age. The crew at C.S.I. had nothing on me!

Sure enough, the goddess appeared. She stood there toweling herself off and checking herself in the mirror and I thought, *Am I the only one seeing this? There must be someone else on the balcony catching this view*, but there was no one.

I then made the biggest mistake a guy in my situation could possibly make. Rather than just keeping this vision of beauty to myself, I told the rest of the idiots I was living with. "Hey guys, you're not going to believe this."

As the rest of the crew slowly piled out to the balcony, one by one, it became like a scene out of a Three Stooges movie, each one of us shoving the other for the best view. We had Doug filling in like a director of a porn movie, telling her which part she should dry off next. I kept reminding them to keep their voices down, as I realized that, if anyone figured out what we were doing, it would probably not bode well for us continuing to live at the condo. But how inconspicuous did this look? Four young construction guys standing on a balcony looking at one window for twenty minutes. Gee, that doesn't look suspicious at all!

I then had the presence of mind to come up with the theory that she must be on a weekly shift and would probably go through the same routine on a nightly basis. To my pleasant surprise, I was right. We would all keep an eye out for this beauty to come home and, sure enough, we all piled on the balcony, rain or shine. The gong show started when one of the guys told someone from the other trades, and pretty soon we had electricians and framers showing up to watch the show. I still can't believe that balcony held all of us up.

I can just see the headlines now: "Peeping Tom Construction Crew Falls to Death Off of Chilliwack Balcony."

Eventually, one of the neighbors must have figured out what we were up to and told her about the fan club. The next day the blinds were drawn tight in the opposite direction, and the fun was over. I felt rather sad, like I had been in a relationship and just got dumped. You know the feeling, the "It's not you, it's me" excuse that leaves you thinking, "What did I do wrong?" Anyway, she started a different shift and we no longer saw her. It was a nice distraction from the fact I was slowly starting to miss the comforts of being in a relationship and having some privacy in my own world.

The local nightclub in the area was called Earthquake Annie's. This place had to be one of the best clubs I had ever been to, if the objective was meeting women. My assumption was this: we were out in the Valley and most of these women were used to seeing guys show up with dirty jeans and ball caps on. I guess they felt privileged if the dude bothered to shower before he showed up. The conversation may have been a bit on the lacking side, as well. So I made sure when I went there, I put some effort into my clothes and my appearance. A little cologne and gel in the hair, and I was pretty much the Brad Pitt of the club with not much competition. That same look was a dime a dozen at the local clubs in downtown Vancouver, but this was Chilliwack. Anything above looking like a farmer and you were an instant hit. We started to spread the word to the friends back in town about the amount of woman we were meeting and soon planned a Friday night with the whole gang out there.

The plan was for us workers to go back home right after the work day was done, get showered and changed, and meet back at John's place. John had the coolest car. We used to call it the Banana Boat. It was an old yellow Pontiac Parisian John had fixed up and muscled out. This car was a convertible and could easily hold six, so we piled in the whole crew, including a couple of our buds, Gordo and Brian. Gordy didn't drink much, so he decided to be the designated driver. The six of us enjoyed a great ride out to the country on a summer night with the top down and the tunes blasting. CDs had just come out, and we thought they were the greatest thing since sliced bread. Anyway, we get to the club and it's hoppin'. We were partying the night away, and I couldn't help but notice John and Doug were getting pretty heavy into the Jack Daniels. I had seen John get a little strange when he got into the whiskey, but I was not prepared for what was about to transpire that night.

I also noticed there was this rather nice-looking brunette giving me a smile from across the dance floor, so I left the gong show to pursue other endeavors. I started chatting her up with my usual bevy of compliments and witty retorts, and soon she was putty in my hands. We were hangin' out getting to know each other, and she asked me back to her place. I agreed but wanted to stay awhile to spend time with the gang.

Last call was soon upon us and I couldn't help but notice John was in his usual whisky state, where he liked to get chirpy and wrestle anyone who would join him. Not really a good hobby to take up when you only weigh a hundred and sixty-five pounds soaking wet. He decided to pick on Doug, who was taking it in stride, but one could see he was getting rather annoyed with John. He also outweighed him by about thirty-five pounds. They turned up the ugly lights and kicked everyone out. We had some cold pops in the trunk of the car, and as we proceeded to have a couple more to cap off the evening, the fireworks started.

John and Doug began to wrestle in the parking lot. Doing this on the grass might not have been such a terrible idea, but on the pavement? This just had disaster written all over it. I remember telling Gordy, where the hospital was, in case anyone should need it. Turns out, this was a wise decision.

The two drunks continued playing WWE wrestling, and eventually Doug got pissed off. I remember him throwing John down to the ground and hearing the eerie thud as a skull hit the ground. John was screaming in pain, and the blood began to trickle down his forehead. What a mess; so much for fun in the country! But rather than the two clowns calling it a night, John decided to start walking away.

Where the fuck does he think he's going? I thought to myself. *We're in the middle of the country.*

As we went after him to talk some sense into him, and maybe get him to a hospital for stitches and check for a concussion, he starts yelling like a wild man and begins to run.

"Where the hell's he running to?" I yelled.

We all figured he just needed to cool down. We assumed he would return soon, so continued to drink our beers and make the best of an awkward situation.

The whole time this is going down, I have my arm around this little cutie I had met. God only knows what she must be thinking at this time. She asks me again to go back to her place and, after watching this circus act, I was ready to do so.

I always tried to play things smart and quickly realized I did not know this girl at all, even though she seemed nice enough. I thought it a wise idea to give Gordy this girl's address and phone number—cell phones did not exist yet—so he could maybe swing by and pick me up in a couple of hours when John returned. I figured I could spend this waiting time a little more wisely, if you know what I mean.

I remember getting back to her place. As I began to look around the walls of the house, there were family pictures of kids and what appeared to be a significant other. She offered me a drink, and one thing started to lead to another. She asked me what I did for a job, and I proudly told her I was an aspiring plumber. I explained the crew of nut jobs at the club consisted of guys from work. I then asked her the same question. She stated she was also in the trades, a roofer, and what a beautiful tan she had. I think I asked her to show me her tan lines, or something to that effect. It worked, and pretty soon the clothes were off.

Things were starting to get rather hot and steamy, and although I was enjoying this whole process, I found it hard to relax, as I continued to take in pictures all over the living room of this mystery guy. Was this just an old boyfriend? If so, why did she still have his picture everywhere? And whose kids were those?

The curiosity got the best of me, so I asked her about the kids.

"Oh, those are my two boys," she explained.

I then asked the obvious next question. "And the guy in all the pictures?"

She paused and said "Oh, that's my husband."

HUSBAND! What the hell?

Well, talk about ruining the moment. I could feel parts of me go limp, and I'm not talking my wrist here, folks. "Your what?" I asked.

"My husband, but don't worry, he took off a couple of days ago and I don't think he's coming back."

I explained to her it was the part where she stated she didn't THINK he was coming back that made me a little apprehensive about continuing with this endeavor. No sooner had I said this when there was a loud knock at the door.

Sweet Jesus! I thought to myself. *It's the husband and here I am in the middle of the living room with my pants down.*

I don't think I have ever put them back on so fast to this day.

We both looked at each other, and I asked if she was expecting company. She said no and went to answer the door. To my pleasant surprise it was my buddy Gordy, our designated driver for the night. He apologized for interrupting, but said he needed to talk to me. I knew I should really get the hell out of there, so quickly said my good-byes and took off with Gordo and the rest of the crew. Only problem was, the crew was missing an important person; JOHN!

"Where's the boss man?" I said.

Gord said that's what he wanted to ask me. "Have you heard from him at all?"

I said no, and I could see the look of concern on everyone's face.

After I had left the bar, he did not return to the parking lot. He just ran his way into the night and was not heard of again. The guys had already checked with the local hospitals, the local police stations, and all his close friends. No one knew where he was, or if he was dead or alive.

By this time the sun was starting to come up, and we could see no other option than to head toward home. We started the car toward the local freeway, and I stated to Gordy that the direction where he started running would have taken him straight to the freeway entrance. John and I had been on the cross-country running team back in elementary school, so I knew he could run a hell of a long way before he got tired. But all the way to the freeway?

John was living with his folks at the time, and I asked if anyone had phoned to tell his parents of our concern. They hadn't, but we all agreed we were now getting desperate for answers, and that it might be time to get his folks involved and make a decision to put out an all-points bulletin with our local police.

We agreed to phone them, and somehow I was voted to make the call. We stopped at a gas station with a phone booth and I dropped in my dime, plus extra for the long distance call. The phone rang, and a rather sleepy mother answered the phone with that slight tone that says, "Who the hell is calling at this ungodly hour?"

I sheepishly said hello and began the conversation. I had known John's mom for many years now, and she actually seemed happy to hear from me. I did not want to alarm or panic her, so I casually stated I knew it was a crazy question to ask at five in the morning, but I needed her to go downstairs and see if John was home.

She inquisitively wondered why he wasn't with us. I kind of gave a nervous laugh as I just said it was a long story, but if she could just pop her head in John's room to see if he was sleeping, we would really appreciate it. She agreed to. I heard the creaking of his door opening and was preparing the speech on how to tell a mother we did not know where her child was. But she returned to the cordless phone and said, "Yes, he's lying in bed. What's this all about?"

I remember feeling a wave of relief when I heard he was home. I answered her question by saying it was the craziest story and I was sure John would fill her in on the details.

"Do you think you could wake him and put him on the phone?"

She did so, and I had the pleasure of talking to Mr. "I can't handle my whiskey."

After I explained the boys had looked for him all night, he laughed as if to say, "Ah, don't worry about me; I'm always fine!"

Turns out, he ran all the way to the Trans-Canada Highway and started hitch hiking. A friendly trucker had spotted this skinny kid with blood all over his face trying to hitch a ride. I'm thinking he must have looked like he just crawled out of a bad accident, or was running from Jason in one of those well scripted *Friday the 13th* movies. Anyway, the trucker drops him off at the exit nearest to his parents' place, and he ran home from there. To put it into perspective, John would have had to run approximately twenty kilometers—twelve and a half miles—to the freeway and from the freeway back to his parents. No small feat, even if one was sober. But our hero did it stinkin' drunk, looking like an extra in a Michael Jackson *Thriller* video.

He asked if the car was okay and where we were. I explained the Banana Boat was well, and we were in a gas station in Chilliwack. He tells me he feels good and wanted us to drop the car off at his place as soon as we could. He then asked if I was interested in working that day. He wanted to get caught up on some of the vent piping on our job site.

"You are absolutely out of your fucking mind dude!" I believe was pretty close to my answer.

I explained Gordy would be dropping us all off, then dropping off the Banana Boat before proceeding home. None of us had received a minute of sleep, while "Jack Daniels" had been sawing logs in his bed all night.

I hung up and told the guys the story. They were all pretty shocked, but I think the general feeling was relief John made it home. Somehow, I don't think we were overly surprised at the outcome though. John was just one of those guys who always landed on his feet against all odds. I don't know if it was skill or just shit house luck.

I do remember showing up for work on Monday, and all the cast iron venting was done. He had actually made good on his word and showed up for a day's work after this whole ordeal. Wow! Yes, life with John was never a dull moment.

Chapter 5

Finding My Way

We soon had the Chilliwack job done, and it was nice to finally be working closer to home. It was also nice to know I had a steady pay check coming in with the promise of a new career.

I must admit, having the approval of Mom and Dad didn't hurt things either. At this point in life, I was once again living in the basement of my parents' place. Rob was not able to find part time work—or did not want to—and I guess his parents were tired of helping him with his part of the rent. It was fun while it lasted.

I've seen him once since then, quite a few years ago when he was back in town to visit his parents. At that time, he had met a lady at a buddy's wedding. She was up from Iowa and the two of them hit it off. He was spending as much time down south as he could with her, and I guess, eventually, decided to marry her and live down there. Wherever he is I hope he is doing well, and I hope his new bride is getting used to his wet piles of laundry and the dirty dishes.

We started a new job in White Rock that would be about a third of the distance I had been travelling. It was to be a concrete, three-floor, prestigious building right on the shores of the Pacific Ocean. I think there were six luxurious suites in total; it was pretty high-end stuff.

The bonus of that job was seeing the view every day. Wow! If you've ever walked the pier in the White Rock area of Greater Vancouver, you know what I speak of. The owner was this old fart named Paul. He hated me because I was not the well-spoken, yacht driving, preppy school boy he thought all young men should be. This guy was always bitching or complaining about something. His son was the general contractor on the job; his name was Mitchell. Mitchell was a good guy, and although you could tell he was trying to fit into the realm of what his father thought he should be, he wanted to be more like us. He enjoyed sticking around on Fridays and having a few beers with us. It was interesting to see the true Mitchell when his dad had gone home.

One Friday, John tells us the company's getting busy and needed more guys. Apparently, he had hired two new plumbers: a journeyman and a second-year apprentice. They would be starting on Monday. I asked what their names were, and I remember him saying Dave and Dwayne.

"Dave and Dwayne?" I said. "That sounds more like a comedy show than a couple of plumbers."

We all had a chuckle at that one, and it turned out to be a rather interesting Monday to start the week. The building was at the point where the concrete floors were poured, and the steel studs were just starting to go up. For the most part, you could see another guy working on the other side of the complex.

I remember meeting Dave just before coffee break, but I still hadn't met this Dwayne guy. I remember thinking to myself Dwayne wasn't a very common name. I had a cousin named Dwayne, but I hadn't seen him since I was a kid. I wouldn't know what he looked like if I seen him on the street. Anyway, this Dwayne was working about forty feet from me with a concrete chipper.

For anyone who has used one of these beasts, you know they are very noisy and you have to keep an eye on what you're doing. I was curious to see who this new guy was, so I kind of glanced at him now and then, but it was hard to see the guy with his head in a hard hat and his face vibrating with the chipper. Eventually, John comes up to talk to him and introduces the two of us. We exchanged pleasantries and soon got back to work.

We eventually all met for lunch and, suddenly, I heard Dwayne laugh. I had a flashback to being a kid at our grandparents' home in the country. Yes, that Dwayne laugh had a ring to it, and I could not help but think, *Could it be? Could this be my cousin I haven't seen in years?*

Of course not, what are the chances of that? I'm going to look like an idiot if I ask the guy in front of everybody, and I end up wrong. I figured it would be like knowing a guy named Steve Smith. You meet another guy with the last name of Smith and ask him, "Hey dude, do you know my buddy, Steve?" Of course he doesn't, because there are a million fucking Steve Smiths in the world, half of them probably in Canada.

I decided to just get to know this guy a bit more. We had a chance to talk a bit later that afternoon. After a few more minutes, I was convinced. It had to be him. I broke the tension by asking about his mom, who would, of course, be my aunt.

Note to self: in future, asking a guy you don't know about his mother is not a good idea. Dwayne kind of took the defensive and, with a rather pissed off, inquisitive voice, asked me why I wanted to know about his mother. You would have had to see Dwayne, a man with a closely shaved head, about six foot two, and solid as a rock. Not the kind of dude you want to piss off.

When I told him his mom's name, he stopped what he was doing and I honestly thought this guy was going to drop me. The look on his face soon turned when I smiled and said I knew the name because she was my aunt. "I'm Kevin Batch, your cousin."

I think the next words were, "Shut the fuck up!"

We gave each other a quick hug and tried to remember how long it had been since we had seen each other. We spent that Friday after work hanging out at his girlfriend's place, having some beers and catching up. It was good to see him again, and he invited Dave to drop by. I actually ended up hanging out more with Dave as the weeks went on, but it never ceases to amaze me how small the world really is.

The White Rock job ended and, if I remember correctly, so did Dave and Dwayne. I think they quit for better paying gigs, but I can't really remember. Faces come and go quite often in the construction trades.

I heard recently from my dad Dwayne is now married and running a personal business of some kind; apparently, he got out of the plumbing trade.

Years later, I was quite shocked when, at my local plumbing wholesaler, in walks this tall guy with short hair. He taps me on the shoulder. It was Dave! I barely recognized him. Dave used to have the long, blonde, Fabio hair that all the chicks loved. Now he's got it cut short. That's not all he's got: he also has a wife and kid, and now runs his own plumbing business. It ends up that he lives about five minutes down the road from me, and we pass work on to each other, even to this day. Like I said, small world.

We then started a much bigger project in the municipality where we all lived, a place called Burnaby. It was a ten minute drive for all of us; all of us except for Fred, that is. He lived in Chilliwack, remember, so now the shoe was on the other foot.

Fred and I were still not getting along very well, and we just kind of stayed out of each other's way. What used to piss me off the most was that on a job site, things are designated through rank, just like in a police station or in the army. My point being Fred was now a fourth-year apprentice, and I was a first year. It was always difficult to take orders from a guy you did not respect, not to mention a guy you thought had the intelligence of a sack of hammers. But soon enough, I would be back in school for my second year and ready to progress to the next level.

Speaking of school, I should touch briefly on that.

We are truly blessed here in southern British Columbia. Not only do we have the ocean, beautiful women, and snow-capped mountains, we also have a world renowned trade school called the British Columbia Institute of Technology.

At the writing of this book, it is still classed as one of the best trade schools, not just in Canada, but in the world. And the beauty is it's located five minutes from my parents' place, where I was living.

There are usually quite a few guys in there from out of town, having to stay at hotels. Some guys were young and single; others had a wife and kids. I always thought that had to be pretty tough. It's not so bad when you are working in a camp making huge money, and the company flies you back home for a few days at their expense. But, this is a situation where you earned peanuts on a government subsidy, and no one was paying for a flight home to see loved ones. Lots of guys have had to sacrifice to get their trade tickets. (Please keep this in mind next time you wonder why tradesmen charge so much.)

I remember the last time I had schooling at BCIT. It was for that high-tech math course I had to take for drafting/engineering in my old life. I hated that, but this was a whole different aspect. I was with a completely different group of people, taking courses I actually was interested in and knew something about. The facilities were quite impressive.

I learned many different facets of the plumbing trade, including arc welding. I have never had to use it, but I have a new appreciation for it. It takes a lot of talent to make a good clean bead, and it's a tough, dirty job.

You meet many different types of guys in the school as well, especially the guys from the outskirts. These are the guys from the smaller towns, usually around northern B.C., and man, do they know how to party. I'd tell some of those stories, but most of them are a bit of a blur!

I did meet some quality people in my first couple of years. Most I have lost touch with except for one, my buddy Kenny.

He sat in the row ahead of me in second year, and I'll always remember him looking back at me saying, "Hey, you a Canucks fan?"

He was referring to our local NHL hockey team, the Vancouver Canucks. I have been a fan since they came into the league back in 1970. I promptly replied I was and we instantly hit it off.

We ended up going to a game a few nights later. Our beloved team was blown out seven to one, but the beer was cold and we had a lot of laughs getting to know each other. We ended up doing our final year together, as well, and received our journeyman papers at the same time. He was best man when I married my first wife, and I was the first person he called when his dad passed away. We have shared some good times. He also introduced me to a weekly get together called "Wine Break," of which I will get into a little later. We now both own property in B.C's Cariboo region, where we go to relax and fish. Although we are not as close as we once were, I hope when life's ups and downs mellow out a bit, we can get our friendship back where it used to be.

Finishing my second year of plumbing school was harder than I expected. I never realized there were so many things a plumber had to know. Trust me, there are things that, to this day, I have never used, but you have to know them, and that's just the way it is.

I returned to the jobsite with John-and Fred-and had a new sense of confidence. I was now halfway to my journeyman's certificate and had a good grasp on the basics of the trade.

At this time, I was still getting jobs that were challenging and took skill, for the most part. I always took this as meaning John was confident in my skills and could see me as an asset to his dad's company. This makes you want to be a solid employee, doing what needs to be done. I had received invitations up to the family cabin during the summer, and also received a beautiful turkey, bottle of Crown Royal, and a nice, fat bonus check for the last two Christmases.

I started to figure it was now time to push my weight around a little. After all, I had been with the company for over two years, and John and I had known each other since kindergarten. This meant I was not going to tolerate any more of Fred's bullshit.

I began to challenge him when he would ask me to do something. Not in a sense of saying I wouldn't do it, but rather I would suggest a better or more efficient way of getting the job done. I did not do this so much to belittle him, but rather to attempt to show him I was not some peon with little to no knowledge of the job at hand. I had secretly hoped this would spur a mutual respect for one another, but sadly, I was wrong. I would then listen to his ramblings at lunch and started to call him out on things he would say. Quite simply, if I didn't agree with his opinion or if I had heard different facts on a news topic, I made sure I put my two cents in. I noticed John quietly watching this private battle between the two of us and just soaking it in, almost the way a hockey coach studies game tapes, or a chess master thinks of his next move.

A specific example I remember was a debate involving heat transfer. He was trying to quiz me as to what I was able to grasp from my second-year schooling. This was, of course, in front of the crew and John, the boss.

He asked me, "So, Kevin, when you're soldering fittings, which end should you start at?"

The correct answer is it doesn't matter whether you start at the lowest fitting or the highest fitting. What they try to teach you in trade school is that most heat rises. Therefore, the right answer, in theory, would be to apply your torch to the bottom area of fittings, allowing the heat to rise to the top area. Heat rises only in radiant type applications. Heat in the air will always travel up. Heat through any medium will always disperse evenly, as in the case of applying a flame to a piece of metal, your heat will disperse equally in all directions.

When soldering, your solder will always travel toward your flame. This is how to control the solder flow and create a good weld.

I had figured this out quite some time ago, but Einstein here was trying to tell me different. When I explained my side of it, he replied, "Well, Kevin, that's just what they told us at trade school, but I guess you know more than them. They should just give you your journeyman ticket now."

I looked at John to back me up but he said nothing. He knew damn well I was right, but I guess he took the higher road and did not want to embarrass Fred. Looking back now, he made the right call, but I sure wanted to know whose side he was on. It must have been hard for him because he had me as a new guy, ready to take on all challenges, but he also had this simple, hard-working family guy who was admittedly honest and always on time. Fred was a good company man and guys like him are hard to find. He was also the higher-ranked guy, so for John to call him out would have been disrespectful. But I still knew if push came to shove, I would be John's boy and he'd stand by me. Or so I thought.

It all came to a head one morning when I was working with Fred in the underground parking lot. You often see a plethora of cast iron pipes in a building parking garage for all the drains needed for bathrooms, storm drains, etc. The hard part is hanging them by rods secured to the concrete ceiling.

A hammer drill is a special concrete drill that "hammers" in and out at a tremendous speed as it rotates. It is usually a diamond tip drill bit that chips the concrete as you drill into it. Basically, it is extremely noisy, and concrete debris sprays all over you as you are on the ladder putting these holes in. You then hammer in an insert, and then your piece of rod with a hanger the pipe goes into.

Anybody who has done it knows what a shitty job it is. Anyway, Fred and I are doing this alone in this parking garage, when I stop to get a new drill bit. Fred decided this was a great time to tell me what he thought I should be doing. I can't remember the specifics, but he made sure I was going to spend the rest of the day down there doing this dirty, mindless work. I explained to him that wasn't going to happen. I was going to drill the holes for my run, and then do my piping. He laughed as he stated that he was the senior man and that I was drilling holes; he was going to do the piping.

I probably made some smart ass comment–who knows–but as I mumbled under my breath he proceeded to look around the parking garage.

47

What's he looking for? I thought. Then I saw the look in his eyes. He was making sure no one else was around. This was not going to be pretty.

He proceeded to slam his hammer drill to the ground and get off his ladder. He then made a beeline for mine. Now remember, this guy's an ex-logger and I'm still a pretty skinny kid at this time. He could have wiped the floor with me, and it looked as though he was about to do so.

I have often heard of the fight or flight scenario psychologists talk of. This definitely flashed in my head, but it's hard to run when you're on a ladder. Upon realizing he was ready to do battle, I quickly got off my ladder–to do what, I don't know. He came at me with his fists clenched, and these were huge meat paws, ladies and gentleman. I decided to stand my ground. Was he really going to get physical on a job site? It would be his termination from the company, for sure.

Maybe I should let him take that swing at me, just enough to fatten a lip. That would be all I would need to never have to deal with this clown again. I stepped back a few feet from the ladder. I had taken karate for a few years just before graduating high school, so I knew how to defend myself. The only problem is a good big guy will beat a good smaller guy every time. Did this guy know how to fight?

He stormed at me and, with a forceful shove, he tossed my wooden ladder to one side. This was an eight-foot ladder, which probably weighs about eighty pounds, and he tossed it like a rag doll. Was I next? He made a fist about two inches from my face and said, "Are you going to do what I tell you?"

I said nothing. I can still see that look on his face, the one where you know a guy is over the edge and not all there mentally. A few fries short of a happy meal, if you know what I mean.

Thank the good Lord he never decided to unleash the right hook. Suddenly, as if better judgment took over, he turned his back and just started walking out toward his truck. Was he getting a gun or other form of a weapon? Okay, now I was getting paranoid. I don't remember what he did after that, but I quickly looked around to see if anyone had witnessed this; there was no one.

I must admit, I was pretty rattled and had a bit of the shakes. It was pretty obvious this could not go on much longer; one of us was going to snap and it would not end as peacefully as this one did.

I decided to deal with this immediately. This would be my opportunity to talk to John and see where I stood in the company. Fred's behavior was obviously not professional and, surely, John would have to reprimand him in some way, shape, or form.

As I made my way to John's work area, I carefully planned my words, as I wanted to be sincere, but not sound like a whiney, sniveling little bitch. I found him and asked if I could speak to him privately for a moment. He agreed and asked me what was up. "You look a little pale; did something scare you down there in the dungeon?"

"Actually," I said, "something did, as a matter of fact."

I proceeded to explain what had happened in the most professional way I could. I tried to pass it off as no big deal, hoping he would respect me even more. But to my absolute astonishment, his reaction to the incident was as follows.

"You know, Kevin, I'm really tired of this bullshit between you and Fred. If the two of you don't start getting along, one of you is going to be leaving. I think you can figure out who that person will be."

Did I just hear that right? I thought to myself. John just walked away from me like I was a twelve-year-old child telling his father that his little brother won't stop poking him. This was a huge violation of professional conduct and I was being made to look the bad guy.

This was the guy I had been friends with since I was five; gone to Beavers, Cubs, and Scouts with; ran on the cross country team with; played soccer and softball with; his family and mine were good friends. To say I was shocked at his response would be a dramatic understatement. When I returned to the underground parking area, Fred was there working and did not say a word to me. I, too, continued to work and did not say a word to him. We finished the day and, at the end, nothing was spoken of, not even by John. It was almost too quiet, like the calm before the storm. The next few weeks would be interesting. Would Fred be moved to another job? Would I be moved? Would I be fired? After John's reaction, anything was possible.

I remember losing a lot of respect for John that day. Here is the guy I would have gone through a brick wall for; the guy I looked up to for years and wanted to emulate. But now, I began to see him in a whole new light. He didn't deserve my praises or accolades. Perhaps he was not the person I made him out to be.

Chapter 6

Coming Into My Own

I guess word had got around the job site about the incident with Fred, and I really don't know if anyone but me cared. I don't enjoy fighting with people. Anyone who knows me usually likes me, as I like to think I'm a very honest and giving person. I almost take it personally if someone doesn't like me. Anyway, about a month after the incident, John tells me Fred is leaving for another job. I wanted to crack a big smile and offer my hand for a high five, but decided to play it low.

John says, "I guess that makes you pretty happy, eh?"

I thought quickly and said, "Well, John, not really. What's best is what's good for the company, and I know Fred was one of your best workers. Why is he leaving?"

John proceeded to tell me his reason was his travel to and from Chilliwack really took away from his family time. He had an offer to start with a small company closer to where he lived. They seemed like pretty legit reasons to me, but deep down we both knew the catalyst that started all this was the incident between him and me.

John was looking at me with disgust and contempt. He was actually blaming me for this. He said something to the effect of me getting what I wanted, and then he proceeded to go back to work. This is one of those moments were you realize you have won the battle, but you can see you will probably lose the war. I had somewhat succeeded in getting rid of one of the biggest pains in the ass I had ever worked with, but at the same time my boss and good friend of over twenty years was looking at me like I was Judas. I was not feeling good about this at all.

I started concentrating my social time with other guys on the job site. I remember getting to know this framer named Dick. He seemed like a nice enough guy, as big as a damn oak tree. I would say about six foot six, maybe two hundred and forty pounds. He kind of took a liking to me, and I guess he had caught wind of the soap opera between Fred and me.

Being a young, naïve kid, I never really knew my role. I would often walk around with my head down, like I was looking for spare change. I did not walk with purpose or confidence. It was pretty easy for the tougher tradesman to get under my skin if they wanted to.

Workers on job sites are a lot like animals in the wild. The pack will pick out the weakest one and focus in on him. I'm not kidding; that's the mentality. If you show weakness, the gang will pick on you and make you the brunt of every joke. An interesting incident happened to me that was one of the best life experiences I have ever had.

I remember being in a far corner of the building in a room by myself. I was installing the metal shell cabinets that hold the copper pipe for baseboard heating systems. It was coffee break, but I did not really want to sit around and bullshit with my crew. I thought my time was better served working. I was learning more and didn't really want to talk to John anyway.

Everyone was in their private vehicles, or construction shacks on lunch, and I was all by myself in this room with no one around. No one would hear me if I yelled for help for an emergency. You should always work with a buddy or have someone know where you are, especially when working with electrical or dangerous power tools.

Suddenly, in walks my "buddy," Dick.

"Hey, Dick," I said. "How come you're not having lunch?"

He looked at me kind of strangely and said he heard some hammering going on; he wondered who it was.

"Ya, just me," I said.

He then proceeded to start talking some bullshit about whether I had a girlfriend or not. Then something about hearing a rumor that I liked men. I assumed this was just good natured ribbing, but I started to get a little weirded out. I was in the corner of a room about ten by ten feet. He was standing in the doorway and, with the size of him, he took up the entire doorway, pretty much. He started calling me a pretty boy and blowing me kisses. Was this guy being nice to me on the job site because he had secretly been gay and was hitting on me?

Now, I was getting nervous and did not like the looks of this situation. "Where is this going, Dick?" I asked.

"I think you know exactly where this is going. Right where you want it to go, sweetie," was his reply.

This is when you really have to man the fuck up and set it straight. The decision of just walking away was not really an option. There was no way I was getting past him. He was serious. This sick bastard was being nice with me on the job, so he could make his move on me. Pick out the smaller one in the crowd, the timid one, and prey on him.

I thought quickly and told him I had to get back to the tool shed for more supplies.

"You're not going anywhere. There's no one here but you and me, and no one's going to hear you scream for help."

I kept waiting for the punch line to end this bad joke, but it just wasn't coming. This guy was nuts. He started walking toward me, and my knees started to literally shake.

All of a sudden, things started to go into slow motion. I guess adrenaline takes over and you just get the courage to do what you have to. As scared as I was, I looked around for any type of a weapon, and there it was at my feet.

I had a large framer's hammer with me and something called an awl. An awl is like an ice pick, only with a large, hard ball on the end so you can strike it with a hammer. I was using this to pierce into the drywall, attempting to find the studs behind the wall to attach baseboard cabinet.

There's a scene in Bruce Lee's *Enter the Dragon* movie, where he looks at the scratch of blood on his chest and then looks at his enemy. He goes into his stance, puts his hand out, and motions for his opponent to come over, as if to say, "Come here; I am now going to kick the living shit out of you!"

This was my look as I swung the hammer around like a pair of nunchuk sticks in my left hand, and the eight-inch awl propped back in my right. I looked at him and, with an almost confident smile, I said, "Unless you want this ice pick to carve your fucking eyes out, I suggest you step back. I'm in no mood for your bullshit."

He stopped in his tracks, looked at me, and began to smile. He nodded his head and said, "You're finally starting to get it. Don't let anybody push you around. Start having some confidence in yourself. If you don't, these guys will walk all over you. You're a smart kid; you're well spoken. These guys will walk all over you if you let them, so don't."

I realized he was just trying to teach me a lesson. I'm not quite sure I approve of the method in which he delivered it, but I certainly got the point.

Dick became like a dad to me on the job site. He didn't let anyone push me around. I've never forgotten that day—hell, would you? It has most definitely come into play many times in my life. There are those who want to see how far they can push you. If you're weak, they'll walk all over you. But stand your ground and many of them pull back. That's not to say you treat people like assholes and walk around like a belligerent prick with a chip on your shoulder. It simply means to walk softly, but carry a bit of confidence, and don't be afraid to use it if you have to. This remains one of the best lessons I have learned in business—and life in general.

It was not long after this the office decided we needed another plumber on the job site. They had hired this new guy who was in his early fifties who was fat and not very social. Don't remember his name, but I caught wind he was going through a divorce. I noticed a few times he had booze on his breath when he showed up for work in the morning.

At that point in my life, I had not been through a divorce, but I could imagine it was not a pleasant thing to go through. Perhaps drinking excessively could be overlooked, until he decided to mess with me.

It was at the end of the week, and we were all sitting at our makeshift shack in the parking garage having a few beers. He conveniently remembered he had forgotten all his tools on the third floor and, in front of all the crew, told me to go up and get them. I looked at him in disbelief and laughed it off, assuming he was joking. He looked at me and said once again, this time with a rather loud voice, "I said go up to the third floor and get my fucking tools . . . NOW!"

I was in shock at this statement and looked at John for some sort of direction. Once again, I was demoralized by someone I used to think was my friend. John proceeded to say because the new guy was a journeyman, and I was merely an apprentice, I had to do as he said and get this fat fuck's tools.

To me, the correct response from John should have been to tell this guy to get his fat ass up to the third floor himself, but it was becoming quite obvious I had fallen out of John's good books, and I was being shown the door in a very casual way. If there was a shitty job that had to be done, John was now choosing me to do it. I began to feel as though it was some kind of punishment for Fred choosing to quit.

At this moment, for the first time, I felt like telling John were he could stick it. Honestly, he was allowing this new guy, who had been with us for a week, to humiliate me in front of the crew. Some friend.

Nobody said a word as I slowly got up. My intention was to start walking up to the top floor for the tools, but it appeared fat ass thought I was getting up to challenge him. He snapped up off the milk crate he had been sitting on, and like a young Clint Eastwood, lit up a cigarette and said, "I'm going to ask you one more time; are you getting my fucking tools or not?"

I kind of felt like I was in a bad Western, but I decided to not make a scene. I proceeded up and made two trips to get all his tools, soldering torch, and I even picked up his jacket. I decided right then and there I would not let this bastard get the best of me. Just like that crazy Dick had told me, I wouldn't let these assholes push me around.

The weekend soon passed, and it was Monday morning. We all showed up on time for work except one. Yes, you guessed it, Booze Breath, my new best friend.

I saw him sneak in hoping nobody would notice, and he proceeded to head up to the top floor to start his day. I watched as he entered one of the suites. I was working on the same floor, so I was somewhat keeping an eye on him, scheming as to how I would soon be able to get even for Friday. Well, I'm happy to say some things just fall into place when you're not even expecting it.

It was coffee time, so I dropped my tools and proceeded to the stairs to head back to the shack. I had not seen him leave the suite he was working in, so I knew he was still in there. Something told me to pop my head in to tell him it was coffee, and as I did, he was nowhere to be found. I had been on that floor all morning. I was positive I had seen him go in, and I was also positive he did not leave. Then, I heard what sounded like someone snoring.

Like a good *Scooby Doo* mystery, I followed the sound to the bathroom area. At this point of construction, the walls were up and rough drywall was installed. We had the toilets in as well as the bathtubs. A common practice was to put the cardboard that the tubs came in over the top of the tub to stop pieces of drywall from going down the tub drain, and to keep the tub from getting scratched or chipped. I pulled back the cardboard cover slowly and found our hero.

There he was, in his entire fat, booze-reeking splendor. He was sound asleep, snoring away, evidently sleeping off his hangover from last night. The company was probably paying this guy well over twenty dollars an hour, which in the early nineties was a pretty good wage.

The gods had handed me a gift. I did not wake him. I quietly put the cardboard back on the tub and allowed him to keep sleeping.

This was like one of those MasterCard commercials, and I intended to make sure my ending was going to be . . . PRICELESS! I made my way down to the shack and made sure the whole crew was there having coffee. I got everyone's attention and told them to follow me upstairs.

"This is the cutest thing, guys. I guess a dog needed a place to give birth to her puppies, and I found them all in one of the tubs on the third floor," I said.

The general response was I was full of shit. I told them to come up and see it for themselves. "The female is nursing the pups as we speak."

They all followed me to the top floor, and I motioned for them to all be quiet so as not to disturb them. They all bought it, hook, line, and sinker, as they began to tiptoe into the bathroom.

I walked up to the tub and said, "Well, guys, I don't exactly have a litter of puppies for you, but it's just a matter of time when you've got somebody fucking the dog this bad!"

I flipped off the cardboard to reveal sleeping beauty. It was priceless. He barely moved; I think he was still drunk from the night before. All the guys had a good laugh. I remember looking at John. He had this look on his face that told me he did not approve of my little prank, but I didn't care. I had caught this asshole red-handed and waited to see how the boss man would handle this one.

They sent him home and he never returned. I don't know if he was too embarrassed to show his face again on the job site, or if he was fired. I would have to think they fired him, but the way things were starting to go in this company one couldn't tell. It started to appear that the quality of new guys being hired was, shall we say, lacking. I started to feel as though I was coming into my own. I had more confidence in myself and knew it was only a matter of time until I found a better company to work for with better pay. John and I were not seeing eye to eye, and for the first time, I didn't care.

Chapter 7

Road Trip to California?

The next plumber they hired turned out to be a very interesting guy. His name was Alex and he was my age. If I remember, his background was Ukrainian or, perhaps, Slovakian. I thought I was good at soldering copper pipes, but this guy was a true "water rat." That's the term they give to guys who do nothing but copper water pipe all day.

Alex was good, and he was very fast. He could easily get an entire suite done in a day and had usually started on the next one before quitting time. He quickly became John's little darling, and I figured I should get to know this guy better. I began to learn some of his techniques, and how he was able to work so efficiently. We began to get a good friendship going. We had one thing in common: we loved to party. He was a single guy living at his parents' place. He and I would often grab a few beers after work and talk shop, or talk about our dreams of what we would do if we had more money. We started talking one night about where we would go for our next vacations. I told him I would like to go back down to California.

I had recalled that, quite a few years ago, my family had driven down to see some relatives. We went to Universal Studios and I had a blast. All that Hollywood stuff really impressed me.

He asked me, "Did you go to Disneyland?"

I told him I had been once when I was really small but didn't remember much of it. He proceeded to tell me he had been there a couple of years ago with his brother. "They've got all new rides and shit; the place is just huge. You should see it now," he said.

"I'd love to; that would be an awesome road trip!" I pondered.

I assumed he travelled by plane, but he told me they just hopped in the car and drove.

"How long is the trip?" I said.

Alex told me they took turns driving and made it down in twenty-four hours. At that moment we both looked at each other, and you could see the wheels in our heads begin to move.

"Let's do it!" I shouted.

He just laughed and said, "I'm in!"

The long Easter weekend was the next week, so that would give us Friday as well as Monday off. We decided to take one extra day, Tuesday, which John hesitantly gave us.

At that time if I had asked, it probably would have been a "no." But Alex was now his star employee, so I wisely got him to ask. We worked out the plan to pack after work on Thursday, then I would drive to his place to pick him up, and off we'd go to the border. We would drive all night.

To even think of doing something like this today would be ludicrous, but at that time in my life, it was kind of fly by the seat of your pants. I was driving a Ford Ranger at the time. I had a sponge, fold out mattress I would often use for camping trips; the same one I used in the Chilliwack days sleeping in the living room. It fit perfectly in the back of the box and I had a canopy on the truck to protect us from the weather. It wasn't all that comfortable, but I didn't care; it worked. If we were going to drive straight through without stopping, we would have to take shifts.

I started, and made it down to about the middle of Oregon. I couldn't keep my eyes open any longer, so I pulled over and gave Alex the wheel.

Now, let me explain something about Alex. He was one of those guys where nothing bothers him; he wasn't afraid of anything and tended to be a bit of a loose cannon. Alex proceeded to take the next exit off the freeway and stop in at a local 7-11.

I found out you can actually buy caffeine pills. This was before all the energy drinks had come out on the market; all we had was Gatorade.

I watched Alex gulp down the biggest coffee he could get and proceed to pop a handful of these caffeine pills. Oh great, this guy was wired for sound, and I would be trying to sleep in the back of the box—just me, the mattress, and the canopy.

Thinking about it now, I did not have a seatbelt, so if he had an accident or rolled my truck . . . well, let's just say I wouldn't be here to write this story. I told him not to drive too fast, which apparently fell on deaf ears, and if I needed him to stop I would tap on the window of the rear cab.

So, I get in the rear of the pickup and try to get some sleep. What a foolish idea that was. Apparently, I had A.J. Foyt behind the wheel. Alex was riding the caffeine wave and must have been doing close to a hundred miles per hour, screaming down Interstate 5 to California. He had the radio turned up so loud he couldn't hear me banging on the glass trying to get him to slow down. It was kind of scary back there. You could feel every bump of the road, and it was loud with the run of the tires. It was the middle of the night in late April, so it was not as warm as I had anticipated. I had forgotten about bringing a blanket or sleeping bag, so was rather cold in the back of this missile.

Somehow, I guess I managed to fall asleep, because when I opened my eyes the sun was just cresting over the horizon. I felt somewhat refreshed and definitely hungry. I tapped on the window, and Alex looked at me with that lazy smile. He sort of had that surfer dude smile that always said, "Fuck, am I stoned," probably because he was half the time.

We pulled over and got a quick bite to eat, and I grabbed a coffee. I took over the driving and was surprised to find we were now in the state of California. We followed the signs to Disneyland and ended up getting a hotel in Orange County, five minutes from Disneyland.

It was a warm, beautiful day. We had made the trip, non-stop, in twenty-one hours. I don't know if that's any kind of record, but I know I would be hard pressed to do that today.

The first thing we did was grab a shitload of beer and just hang out around the pool/hot tub area of our hotel. We decided to just chill out for the evening and take in Disneyland the next day. Alex decided he was getting his drunk on. He was one of those guys that would just open up his mouth and pour the beer straight in. Honestly, he would barely swallow. Just open the gullet and pour the beer in. It was not uncommon for him to have a beer done in two minutes, and then be on to the next one. He would have a six-pack polished off before I was cracking my third beer. Unfortunately, I had to do a little babysitting when he got plastered. He was a little unpredictable when he got to the sloppy stage. He wasn't a violent guy, but you could see he would start to give somebody the "stink eye" and I knew it was time to get him out of wherever we were.

The next morning was Saturday and we finally made it to Disneyland. I never realized how massive that place is. I mean, you need a good three days to really see and appreciate all the stuff there. We hit all the rides we could and just soaked it all in. The people, the music, the attractions – everything. We were like a couple of kids, and it felt great to be enjoying the California sunshine.

The final day was Universal Studios. We had a limo taxi pick us up at our hotel and take us back when the day was over. If you haven't been to this place, I highly recommend it. If you enjoy movies and great theme rides, it's the place to be. Too much fun!

We left Monday late morning and headed back for home with a bunch of pictures and laughs. We did not have digital cameras at this time, so we had to take the film in to have it developed. If you were lucky, you would have your pictures back the same day.

We did not time our trip very well, because we hit rush hour on the I-5 coming into Seattle; five lanes of nothing but bumper-to-bumper traffic. Alex realized we could use the H.O.V. lane. We did, and just flew by everybody.

This was the first time I had seen or heard of a separate lane for cars that had more than one person in the vehicle. Now, you see them everywhere; they are quite common here in Vancouver. It astounded me how many Americans do not carpool . . . and how bad their traffic problem is. I shudder to think if that was then, how bad it is now.

We arrived back home mid-afternoon on Tuesday. We took turns driving, but by this time we did not have the energy to race back home at break-neck speed.

Alex and I were back at work the next day and had the radio on as we worked. They interrupted the music to report heavy rioting in the Orange County area of Los Angeles due to the not-guilty verdict for the cops that beat Rodney King. It was happening a few city blocks from the hotel we had just returned from. That would have been an ugly scene, and we both counted ourselves lucky we got out of there when we did.

I bumped into Alex a few years ago, and we spent some time catching up. His boozing was starting to get the best of him, so he quit drinking. He was enjoying his sobriety with his new lady and their first child. He seemed quite happy. I guess we all have to grow up sometime. I wish him well.

Chapter 8

Final Days with John

We soon had the Burnaby job completed, and it was always a question where your next job was going to be. That's one of the problems with doing construction. Once the company you are with has completed the job, there is often a few weeks or even months before the next big job starts. You sometimes have to go out and look for other companies to work for that are busy. That's just the way it is.

John and his dad had two projects underway: one was a small strip mall John was on, the other was an old high-rise building in downtown Vancouver that needed all the old water pipes decommissioned and new ones installed. This also included removal of all the asbestos insulation covering the pipes in the walls.

John had handpicked all his favorite guys for the crew at his mall job. I was demoted to the shitty, labor intensive job of opening the walls to remove the asbestos pipe installation. This isn't a plumber's job; this is a job for a young kid with no experience. That's who I was stuck working with. It was an insult and I definitely got the message. Continuing to do jobs of this nature meant learning nothing of the trade and, therefore, a waste of my time.

They had hired a new guy to run the crew. I can't remember his name, but I personally didn't think he knew what the hell he was doing. They also hired two long haired, chain-smoking teenagers to be the laborers on this new job. I must admit, these two clowns were a laugh a minute. I was stuck working with them, removing the asbestos insulation.

We had a professional hazmat team come in and fit us with respirators and body suits, so we would not come in contact with the dreaded cancer-causing material. I recall one day, the three of us were working on the same floor. We stopped for morning coffee, so I poked my head into the suite they were working in. Keep in mind, these are people's fully furnished condos overlooking the beauty that is Vancouver's downtown west end-the view of the ocean and mountains is breathtaking, and these apartments are worth a fortune.

The occupant was obviously not home. I walked in to find dumb and dumber up to no good. One of them had the TV remote control in his hand and was channel surfing to catch some sports highlights. The other comes wandering out of the tenant's bedroom with a pair of women's underwear and is proceeding to sniff the crotch area. He looked at me like he was doing nothing wrong and said, "Oh hey dude, you want a sniff?"

Where did they find these two delinquents? I shook my head in dis-belief and told them it was coffee break.

Normally, being the senior guy, I would have given them shit, but I think at this point I didn't give a shit. As I took the elevator down to the lower parking garage where our lunch shack was, I thought to myself, *this is fucking ridiculous.* I was soon to go into the third year of my apprenticeship, and I was removing asbestos from walls. What's wrong with this picture?

It was now obvious I was going to receive every shitty job the company had to throw at me. John no longer respected me, and I guess I no longer respected him. This was their way of slowly pushing me out. I had gone from learning the plumbing trade and looking forward to my job, to being a grunt and ripping cancer-causing material from a wall. Time to get the hell out of this gong show. And I soon did, but not without a few hiccups along the way.

I knew I wanted to be my own boss one day and I also wanted to be independent. I knew I had a pretty good knowledge and grasp of the plumbing basics at this point and was bound and determined to get out there and not only prove it, but also make some money.

My confidence was taking a bashing at the hands of John's company. I was starting to feel like I wasn't progressing in the trade or learning anymore. As my dad would say, I was spinning my wheels.

I had done the odd side job with John when days were better between us, and I wanted to get back into that realm of work. Only this time, it would be my jobs and I would be taking in the big money. I put an ad in the local newspaper saying, "Local plumber for hire. Reasonable rates."

I had some basic tools and went out and bought some basic plumbing parts I figured I might need. I had found some old milk crates in my dad's garage and used them to hold my parts. (I still use those same crates to this day.)

I had just purchased my first cell phone, so this was the number I put in the ad. I laugh when I think of the size of that old dinosaur phone, five times the size of the ones today. Does anyone remember the huge phones that were the size of a masonry brick with the big eight-inch antenna? How times have changed.

I've often felt that people would not and do not take you seriously when you drive up to their house in anything less than a professional work van. I was using a black Ford Ranger, and that just reeks low budget and inexperience. They were right.

I received a call and went out to do my first job on my own. I was about to find out doing this type of work was not as easy as I thought; I was about to learn a very valuable lesson.

This married couple had an older home that obviously had some renovations done to it. The upstairs area, where the washer and dryer were, had new hardwood floors put in and looked quite updated.

The problem was that lint from the clothes washer was making it past the filter of the machine and into the p-trap of the drain. (This is the u-shaped piece you often see under a sink.)

There is often a union connection or a small cleanout at the point of the trap, so you can remove it to clean it out. I did so, and when the customer asked me what she could do to stop this from happening again, I tried to come up with a brilliant idea.

I remember reading something in one of those home remedy books about the use of panty hose. Apparently you can use them as a fan belt if you're stuck without one for your car, and I remember it also saying it works as a good screen for filtering fine items.

I proceeded to ask her for an old pair, which is kind of embarrassing in itself. She found one, and I proceeded to duct tape the pantyhose to the end of the water discharge hose of the washing machine.

My idea was the water would be filtered by the pantyhose before it got to the p-trap. I reminded the customer to make sure she cleaned it out once a week, and she should not have any more clogged pipes.

How stupid was this fucking idea? Wow! I still can't believe I was the mastermind behind this failure. I didn't even bother to test this theory first; I just installed it and collected my money.

This was great; my first real job on my own. This was the start of a whole new career, or so I thought. There's an old expression: a fool and his money are soon parted. Isn't that the truth?

Within forty-eight hours, I received a phone call from a very irate husband. He explained who he was and what had happened. Apparently, my pantyhose idea was not the professional breakthrough I had hoped it to be. On one of the discharge cycles of the machine, it pushed the nylon off the end of the hose and into the p-trap. This, in turn, blocked the water flow, causing it to bubble up and out of the pipe, and . . . you guessed it . . . completely flood the upstairs kitchen. What a mess!

This ruined the new hardwood floors and did major water damage to the ceiling below.

The customer demanded their full money back, and I was responsible for the payment of their deductable for insurance. If I did not comply, they were taking me to small claims court.

What a way to start my new business. I obviously had a lot to learn. I went over the next day after work and paid them all the money they asked for. I also apologized for the mess.

At this point, I had to admit I was not ready to run my own business. I still had a lot to learn. But would I learn what I needed to by continuing to work at John's company, where I was going nowhere? Dad always told me to never quit one job until you had another one to start. Good advice, but I did not know where I was going to go. I didn't have enough experience to be a wanted asset to most companies. I was getting there, but not quite.

As I have stated, and will continue to state many times in this book, it is amazing how doors just seem to open and opportunity will knock. Always remember to ensure you pay attention to the paths that come to you.

Enter an old friend of over thirty years now. He was not only a kid I grew up with, but also a plumber in the trade longer than me. A guy I am very proud to say is still one of my best friends to this day.

Ladies and gentleman, allow me to introduce my good friend, Mags.

Chapter 9

My Journey with Mags

Mags isn't his real name; it's an abbreviation of his last name. Everyone in the trade and all his close friends call him Mags, so that's the name we will use for this book.

He's the type of guy other dudes aspire to be like. He has the beautiful wife, the perfectly manicured lawn, the pristine house on the corner lot, and everyone says hello to him when they see him.

I remember going to a hockey game with him to see our local NHL team. We walked into the arena that holds about twenty thousand people, and we couldn't get more than a hundred feet into the door without a couple of people stopping him to say hello. The guy's been body building since he was a teenager and always keeps himself in shape, but the great thing is he doesn't walk around in all the muscle shirts that scream "look at me!"

People respect him because he always has the time for you. Very rarely do you hear him speak badly of anyone. He may think it, but he is always the bigger person and keeps it to himself; a class act if there ever was one.

We grew up just down the block from each other, and as kids we would often get together with the rest of the neighborhood gang and play street hockey. Mags still bugs me when we get together for drinks about the time I "painted" my goalie mask with wax crayons.

I wanted to look cool like my NHL heroes. I knew my dad wouldn't get me the paints or support the idea of defacing my brand new mask they just bought me for Christmas. So, I used what I had, hoping no one would notice it was wax crayons. They did, and I was the laughing stock of the block.

Come to think of it, I was never a good goalie anyway. I remember one shot that deflected off my blocker and right into the next door neighbor's garage. I never knew a tennis ball had that much force, but it smashed through the plastic siding and into his car. (What's funny about this story is that about four months ago, I had a service call in the old neighborhood and, sure enough, that hole is still there to this day.)

Mag's parents still live on that block, and when he goes to visit he often calls me to laugh about the "infamous blocker deflection."

Speaking of that garage, I recall a beautiful sunny day when I was out washing my truck in the back alley of Mom and Dad's place. Coming up the alley was this big station wagon with the wood paneling on the side. *Who the hell is this?* I thought to myself.

Sure enough, it was my buddy Mags. At this time in our lives, we had lost contact. He was living on his own with some roommates and, of course, I was back at home with the folks. I hadn't seen him in quite a few years. I asked him what the hell he was doing back at the old stomping grounds.

"Had to make sure the hole was still in the plastic. Painted anything with crayons lately?" he sarcastically asked.

After asking him if his boyfriend bought that car for him, we had a good laugh and talked for quite some time.

We did the usual "How's your folks?" and so on, but then he asked what I was doing for work. I told him I was slowly working my way into the plumbing trade. He was shocked, and soon explained he was also in the trade and had just finished his schooling. What a complete coincidence that two close friends who grew up together would end up in the same trade. It would eventually lead to us working together for our own companies, but we'll get to that.

I explained I was not happy working with John. After telling him all the bullshit I was putting up with, he told me where he was working.

Mags was in the plumbing union, working on the new arena being built in downtown Vancouver. At the time of its building, it was called GM Place. (Due to GM falling on hard financial times, it is now called Rogers Arena.)

This would be a dream come true for a guy our age. The union was paying good money, even for apprentices, and we would be building the new home of our beloved Canucks. Then he asked the question that ranks up there with, "Would you like the winning numbers to the lotto?" He wanted to know if I would be interested in a job there.

I just about peed myself with excitement when I asked, "Are you serious?"

I called in sick the next day and went straight to the union hall. I paid my first month's dues and did all the monotonous paperwork; I was now officially in the union.

I called Mags to ask what my next step was. He gave me the name of the shop foreman on the job, and I went the very next day. If I remember correctly, they told me they would be in touch with the union hall if an opening came up. I went home with slight disappointment, as I was still stuck in my shitty job.

There is an old expression that says good things come to those who wait. A few days later, I received the call from the union hall telling me my name had been selected for work.

I felt like I really had won the lotto. Although nothing was ever said, there were many other guys looking to get that job, guys that had probably been paying their dues much longer than I had. But, if the company hiring puts in a name request, you get the job. It seems pretty obvious someone at that job site with a good reputation stuck his neck out for me and dropped my name to the boss. I wonder who that could have been? Thanks, Mags!

I did give my two week's notice to John and his dad, because my father always said that was the right thing to do. Kids today just up and quit, but you never want to burn any bridges.

I seem to remember them telling me if I had another job to go to, they would not mind if I left before my two weeks. Were they being polite or just couldn't wait to get rid of me? I guess I'll never know, and I don't really care.

Mags and I decided, since we were both working at the same place, we might as well carpool to work in the morning. He had to go through the old neighborhood anyway, so he picked me up every morning in his chick-magnet station wagon. He actually had a name written on the side of it: Big Bertha. To this day, I don't know what the joke is behind that one. One day, I shall have to ask him.

I was pretty nervous my first day, but Mags introduced me to most of the guys he knew, and I felt more comfortable. I'll tell you one thing: there was certainly a plethora of interesting characters from all walks of life. Allow me to tell you about them.

One of the first guys to say hello to me was this crazy dude who always had his hard hat on—even on lunch breaks—and always had a smoke hanging out of his mouth—even on lunch breaks—and had one lazy eye that looked opposite the side to which he was talking to you. I can't remember his name, but his favorite thing was answering any point you were trying to make. Did I mention that he also had a lisp?

He would answer with, "Well, this is just it, ya see," only it came out, "Well, thith ith juth it, ya thee."

It was hilarious, the smoke hanging out of his mouth and him lisping his way through a conversation. You were never really sure if he was talking to you or the guy beside you, because his eyes were looking at both of you. Sometimes, to this day, Mags will give me a text out of the blue, saying, "Tho this ith juth it, ya thee." It still cracks me up.

There was Billy, the party animal who loved to play cribbage every lunch hour. He was good; not many guys could beat him.

I would head over to his place every time he was having a UFC party. This was when the popular, mixed martial arts contests were just starting out on pay-per-view TV.

There was Mikey, another crazy party guy who was always laughing.

And there was my weird supervisor; everyone called him "Fluffy." Apparently, he went for a different look some time ago, deciding to perm his hair. It was frosted blonde on the tips; he looked like the frayed top of a Q-tip or a poodle fresh from the salon. This gave him the name Fluffy, and it was now permanently affixed. He always reminded me of a guy who was never really comfortable in his own skin. I, for one, never really trusted him.

We even had this make-work project for less fortunate kids at the job site. We had this very inexperienced apprentice who received the job from the government. He was in and out of juvenile detention centers, so the provincial government at the time had a program where they would pay half his wage. A great deal for the company, because this kid was not only useless, he was a pain in the ass to socialize with. He was one of those guys I like to call a "one upper." No matter what story you tell, he knows a guy who has, or he himself has, done one better than your story. The exaggerations become ridiculous and rather than calling him out and embarrassing him, you just try and avoid him. It's funny that even now in my life, I know people much older who are still like that.

This kid ended up lasting only a few weeks, as one day we had an ambulance on site. We all asked if anyone knew what happened. Apparently, the new kid was never taught how to properly close a ten-foot ladder. He attempted to do so, wrongly, and when the momentum of the ladder slammed shut, he had his hand wedged between the mid-span metal support rods. Ouch!

These are rather thin, as they are only there to keep the ladder from twisting in the middle. The momentum must have nearly sheared his hand in two. He did not return to the job site.

One day, they had me working in a trench with crazy Mikey. He was a mess that morning and I figured out why he was always laughing; he was high as a kite all the time!

We had to put together a very large diameter piece of ductile iron for the main water line coming into the building. Mikey had been up all night partying on God-knows-what substance, and he was in no shape to do anything but sleep. One of the old school supervisors, Larry, was just making his rounds.

This guy was a no bullshit, crew-cut type of army sergeant who would rip your ball sack over your head if you bad-mouthed him. He must have been in his early sixties, but nobody messed with him. If you ever get a chance to see the Mel Gibson movie *We Were Soldiers*, watch for the character that Sam Elliot plays; this was Larry.

Since I was the apprentice and Mikey was doing his best to pretend to be a journeyman, I was supposed to be there to give him a hand if he needed it. He was shaking so bad he could barely hold the wrenches, but he still had the smile going.

The bolts and nuts we had to put in the pipe connection were close to an inch and a half in diameter; they took a lot of torque to get them in. Mikey tried to reef on one of them as I was holding the cap, and the wrench slipped. He ripped the top of his hand on the rough lag bolts and was bleeding like a stuck pig. As I gave him a rag to stop the bleeding, the poor bastard started to break down.

"Oooo. Owy. Ooo. Oh. Owey. Owey. Ohh!

He sounded like a five-year-old child that had fallen off his bike.

"Holy fuck, Kev, I was up all night partying. You gotta help me."

I shook my head and said, "Give me the wrenches!"

I proceeded to finish the job when Larry walked over to see what the fuss was about.

"What the fuck's going on here? What's all that fuckin' yelling about?"

I decided to help Mikey, as I kind of got a kick out of him. "Nothing, Larry. Uh . . . Mikey just hurt his hand, so I'm finishing up the bolts. Nothing to see here."

After getting the look that made me think I was going to have to drop and give him twenty, he walked away.

"Holy shit, that was close, Kev. Thanks, buddy." He told me to finish the job as best I could. He then proceeded to crawl into a corner of the trench and put jackets over himself. The bastard slept until coffee while I finished his job.

I realized that being on a union job is quite different than a non-union job in many ways. With many non-union jobs, the pace is go, go, go . . . get the job done as fast as you can and, sometimes, one is persuaded to cut corners if one has to.

A union job is a much slower pace where safety is always first; you have the proper number of journeyman to apprentices on the site at all times, and you are not pressured to finish the job at a quickened pace. In fact, you are cautioned to make sure the job is finished no sooner than the quoted timeframe. This was very different than what I had been used to.

Unfortunately, it also seemed it did not matter how hard you worked or what skills you knew; it was who you were related to or hung out with. The union is very cliquey in this way and that always used to piss me off. It always seemed that even though I showed up on time every day and did my job to the best of my ability, I was treated as a nobody, always receiving the shit jobs.

I don't mean to slam the unions. If it wasn't for the early unions of our grandfather's day, tradesmen would earn far less money today for skills that often are risky and have some sort of health risk accompanied with them. For that, I am grateful.

But I can see that our plumbing union is in trouble. There appears to be too much inner backstabbing and finger pointing within the ranks and too many power hungry people who are not the right men for the positions they hold. But I digress.

I have heard the saying many times that sometimes life is about being in the right place at the right time; it can also be about being in the wrong place as well.

One of my jobs was to core the holes through the concrete floor to make way for water pipes, drain pipes, electrical conduit, and so on. This is heavy work and somewhat boring and monotonous.

I had been on the coring machine for about a week when I had this brilliant idea. Rather than stand up and slowly drill each hole in the floor, I grabbed a five-gallon bucket to sit on. This was much easier on the back and generally made the job easier to do. I never stopped to think for a moment that I looked lazy or was doing anything unsafe. Apparently others did.

It was almost coffee time and I was halfway into a six-inch diameter core hole. I was sitting on my bucket, staring blankly at the coring bit, when a group of suit and ties walked by. They all stared at me. I looked up and gave them a wry smile that probably had a bit of a "What the hell are you looking at?" attitude. I wondered who they were, but passed it off as just another bunch of corporate drones looking at putting some kind of business in the arena.

After coffee I was told to stay behind, as the head foreman of the job site wanted to talk to me. I went into his trailer and said good morning. "Not for you, it's not," was his response.

A cold chill ran over my body. "Uh . . . sorry?" I said.

He asked how the coring was going and if my bucket was comfortable. I explained it was easier on the back, but I did not like where this conversation was going. As it turns out, the suits that walked by were the owner of the plumbing company . . . and the CEO of General Motors of Canada. The rest of the groups were potential investors and associates. The owner had deemed me lazy and not regarding safety for sitting on the bucket.

I was absolutely shocked when I heard this. Just for sitting on a bucket! Are you fucking kidding me?!

I was at the wrong place at the wrong time and, had I known who this group of people was, I obviously would have stood up and looked like I was doing something important. But I didn't, and when the next group of layoffs came, I was gone.

I can't help but think there was more to it, but if that's how they want to run the show, who am I to say any different?

The project was completed in '96, and I have been to many hockey games in GM Place. I remember sitting in the stands one lunch hour when the ice was nothing but a pile of dirt, with welders and iron workers putting in pipes and rebar. I imagined the Canucks playing, with the crowd screaming. I still hope to one day see them raise the Stanley Cup on that ice.

I'm pissed at the way things ended, but I am grateful I had my time to be part of the project.

GO, CANUCKS, GO!

Chapter 10

Leaving the Union for Better Days

I was into my third year of schooling at this point and remember being at the cafeteria one day in line for lunch. We were doing a piping project and, for safety reasons, our instructor requested we bring and wear our hardhat if we had one. Anyone who did not would be issued one.

I had forgotten to take my hat off as I was standing in line. I had also forgotten a very visible sticker was plastered on the back clearly stating I was a "proud" union worker and supporter.

Next thing I know, two very big guys were in line behind me, taunting me and giving me a very bad time. "Look at the big union man thinking he's better than the rest of us."

I turned around to see who was doing the chirping. This guy and his buddy clearly had about eight inches in height and about forty pounds each on me.

I calmly said, "Sorry, what was that?"

He and his buddy verbally laid in to me about how much they despised the union and some of their practices. I had never met these two guys in my life, but they felt strongly enough to display their opinions to me in the middle of a line up at a crowded cafeteria. I explained it was just a hardhat, and that I had my reservations about my union as well.

For the first time, it really made me realize how politics and status can bring out the worst in people. It also made me wonder if this was the path I wanted to continue for my career.

I soon finished third year and was hired to work at the Vancouver International Airport expansion project. Our local airport was greatly undersized for the amount of traffic it was receiving. It was a huge project, and I was brought on with a company from Alberta doing much of the piping for the project. I was once again with a group of guys I did not know and did not have my good buddy, Mags, to hang around with.

I felt as if all efforts I made to fit in or get to know anybody were futile. I never had this problem when I was on a non-union job, but these guys just seemed to have the attitude I was only an apprentice and was worthy of nothing. This could not have been more evident than when they stuck me with this journeyman named Fred.

I could not help but think of the other Fred from the days working with John, and hoped my relationship with this one would be better. It was not to be.

This guy definitely had small man's syndrome, as he was about four foot eight, pretty close to a midget I would say.

I had just been through all the different ways to calculate piping scenarios, as this is taught in third-year plumbing. One would assume the older journeyman should know all these things, since he is the one making the big money and benefits. That was not the case.

Fred, in my opinion, was as smart as a bag of wet dog shit. This guy thought the good Lord said "trains" when he was giving out brains, and this poor bastard missed his.

We had to put this piece of ductile iron water pipe up and attach it to hangers from the ceiling of the building. The ceiling height was about twenty-eight feet. Two guys with ladders and a lift, hauling these pieces of pipe that weigh about fifteen pounds a foot. Needless to say, the pipe is cumbersome and dangerous to work with on a ladder.

We came across a situation where we had two pieces of pipe in the air that did not line up, but needed to be joined. It was a simple matter of applying the Pythagorean theory: A squared + B squared = C squared.

Applying a multiplying factor of 1.414 will give you the distance you need on a forty-five degree angle, as well. This is basic knowledge, so I thought, and would make our job easy.

To my frustration, this clown had me up and down the ladder many times over the course of the day, trying to use a tape measure in the air to get the measurement.

He would give me measurements to cut that always ended up being too short or too long. How much time and money was wasted on labor and the cost of materials? I politely suggested we use the calculation method to work out the length. The answer I was given was as follows: "Who's the fucking journeyman and who's the apprentice here?"

He stormed away from the work area and just took off. What the hell just happened here? Apparently, he went directly to the foreman like a whiney little bitch and complained that he couldn't work with me. Wow! I was just not used to working with this caliber of insecurity. I'm trying to be a team player and help better the situation, and this prick goes to complain about me?

The foreman gave me a "chat," with a warning to hold my tongue. He was a young guy, like myself, and knew the frustration I felt. He and I got along quite well, but it all comes down to rank and job status.

I walked over to a corner and pulled out a small pad and pen I always keep on me. I quickly worked out what the length of this piece of pipe should be, scribbled it down, and stuffed it in my front lapel pocket. I hesitantly apologized to the midget, and we got back to work. We eventually got the piece in by way of trial and error, after about eleven attempts. The final measurement that fit was the same as the number on the paper in my pocket.

I know I shouldn't have done it, but you guessed it. I pulled the paper out to present it to him. I smiled as I looked him in the eye and gave him the paper. "I know I'm just an apprentice, but I wrote this measurement down while you were complaining to the foreman. How much time do you think we would have saved?"

He crumpled the paper, gave me a pleasant, "Fuck you!" and walked away. What? Was it something I said?

It was Friday after work, and some of the guys had driven to the outskirts of the parking areas having a few beers. I was driving by, wishing them a good weekend, when one of them surprisingly waved me in for a beer. I was thirsty, so graciously accepted the offer.

To this day, I can't remember his name, but I do remember the big mustache. You know the type; one quite often sees them in bad porno movies from the seventies.

We got to talking. I had seen him around the job site, and he seemed like a good guy.

"So how are they treating you around here?" he asked.

I did not hesitate to tell him things were less than peachy. I began to discuss the fact I was beginning to do the occasional side job and really wanted to start my own business, once I received my journeyman plumbing ticket. I will never forget his response and still think of it and laugh to myself even today.

"Your own business?" he laughed. "Let me tell you something. My cousin tried to start his own business last year. Quit his job and everything. After getting himself into debt and almost losing his house and marriage, he was begging for his old job back. You better shake your fuck'n head and start kissing ass to the bosses like the rest of us do. You'll never make it on your own!"

Now, I'm the type of person that, if you tell me I can't or shouldn't do something, it makes me want to do it all the more. Like telling a child not to touch something; when your back is turned, they're touching it! It made me feel more incentive to accomplish a successful business, because now it seemed even more dangerous and risky than I first thought.

I began to drop hints to my family and friends that this is what I wanted to do one day. I would like to tell the typical mushy love story that everyone supported me all the way, but it was not the case. My comments usually got me looks of concern and comments of negativity.

So I began to talk to people who were running their own show. Tried to find out how they got started, how they became successful. After all, why reinvent the wheel? Just follow the steps of someone who has accomplished what it is you strive to do.

I believe it was the Monday following that weekend I received my layoff papers. Just as well, I was sick of working there anyway. I began to think about a better future. Hmm . . . if I could only find a job where I could learn the small business end of things. Hmm . . .

Chapter 11

Learning the Ropes

I was now unemployed again. I had made a few phone calls and gone for a few interviews, but they were not what I was looking for.

One Saturday night, me and a buddy are thinking of heading out to catch the game. We chose a popular pub out in the Coquitlam area. Chances were we would bump into someone we knew.

I think I arrived there half in the bag, if you will, and getting a couple more under my belt gave me the liquid courage to ask some of the sexy felines for a dance. Just for the record, I dance like a regular white guy, but after a few conversations with Mr. Bud Weiser I figure I'm Fred Astaire.

I distinctly remember this gorgeous young lady with her friend at the far table. I walked up with my best line and asked her to dance. She immediately told me she was in a relationship, but her friend was single.

The friend wasn't my first choice, but with beer goggles on, hey, I was in. I didn't want her to feel like she was second best, so I used a smooth cover line. Something like, "I was actually going to ask you first, but my friend was interested in you. Oh well, his loss. Let's dance."

Yup, I'm pretty smooooooth!

By the time the evening was done, I had her laughing with my boyish charm and was getting a rather naughty good-bye kiss in the parking lot. I could not help but notice she was driving a nice car, so I ever so gently asked her what she did for a living. She then proceeds to tell me she runs a plumbing, heating, and gas company. I remember thinking, "Wow, this is just too easy."

I asked her to be serious with me. She was.

I believe it was at this point I looked for the TV cameras, figuring I must be on hidden camera. I was waiting for Ashton Kutcher to pop out telling me I was being punked.

"Why?" she said. "What do you do for a living?"

I explained to her I was a plumbing apprentice who was looking for employment. I asked if she was hiring and, with a cat-like smile, she said, "Maybe."

We said our good-byes and I made sure I got her number.

Turns out, her father had an established plumbing company in the Vancouver area for quite a few years. He had passed away from a massive heart attack a few years earlier. She and her mom were now the owners of the company. She answered the phones, did the bookkeeping, and paperwork. The actual plumbing was done by whoever was hired at the time.

A good clientele base is always important to a business, and it appeared her father had some very loyal customers who continued to use the company even though he was no longer alive.

We began dating, and I was soon asked to come to the office to meet the other workers. Since she ran the office from the basement of her home, it was also an opportunity to meet her mom.

The family was Italian. Her mom was rather soft spoken and, let me tell ya, that woman could cook. The best Italian cuisine I have ever had, better than any restaurant. This was a relationship I could definitely get used to.

The head plumber there was a tall, thin guy named Jim. He and I hit it off pretty quick. I still see him around town to this day. We often say we'll get together for a beer, but unfortunately, never have.

84

The other guy, also a journeyman, was Craig. He was a bit of a short guy with a definite small-guy attitude. He called everybody "Mister."

"Hey, Mister, you shouldn't be doing that." His other expression was, "He's a good guy."

These two guys had personalities completely opposite of each other. They got along like oil and water. Funny thing is I got along with them both, but it was always awkward when the three of us got together.

I had a brief interview as to what my experience was, and how much I knew of the service industry. I had done construction work in commercial and industrial, but knew nothing of residential service.

To clarify, *residential* refers to the average person's home. *Service work* refers to fixing broken items, renovations, or small installations, like a hot water tank or new toilet. I was honest in telling them I did not know much in this field, but wanted to learn the business. They also did heating and gas, which I wanted to learn as well.

I got the job—big surprise—and soon began what would be the start of a lifetime career. I still had one more term of school to go, and my next term was starting in a month.

I spent the first few weeks driving around with Jim, just getting to know the customers and watching him do various jobs. The majority of our time was spent drinking beer and playing pool back at the games room in the office. I could not help but notice things were pretty slack and work was not that busy. This was completely opposite from what I was used to. There was not a lot of structure. Some days we worked hard; other days we had one job and went home.

I was now dating the "owner" full time and when things weren't busy at work, she was over at my place.

It would drive me nuts that her cell phone would be going off all the time. Wouldn't be so bad if it was a job being lined up, but it was Jim! "What the hell is his problem?" I would ask.

She would just tell me he was concerned about the various jobs and wanted to keep on top of things. Seemed kind of odd to me, but what the hell did I know about the business?

It was a Friday night after work, and I was going to start school on Monday. Jim and I were having beers at his place when I decided to ask why he felt he had to check in with my girl so often during the day to talk about nothing.

He looks me in the eye and tells me he used to date her. I was shocked and said, "So, like, a few years ago?"

He tells me they broke up just before she met me, and they went out for two years! Wow, talk about awkward!

She would often tell him she was doing something else when she was hang'n out with me. He knew it was bullshit and just wanted to confirm we were dating full time. I told him the truth. I thought there might be hard feelings but, you know, Jim was a good sport, and we had built a friendship even after only a few weeks. We both laughed it off and enjoyed the evening.

I eventually finished my final year of school and was eager to get back to work. I was now getting enough experience to work with Jim and do a few jobs on my own. I would work occasionally with Craig and enjoyed it when I did. He loved to talk hockey and golf, two sports he was very good at, I must admit.

He, like Jim, was eager to give me advice and show me how to do things. The more I worked with him, the more we talked and struck up a good friendship as well. He was a good drinker and loved to prattle on when he got going. I tend to think some of the stuff was bullshit, but who am I to say.

He got me into golfing. That guy could have turned pro if he put his mind to it. I eventually broke one hundred on a consistent basis and still play today. I don't get out nearly as much, but I love golf as a great pastime with the buds.

One night, after a good round of golf . . . and beers . . . we were hang'n out at his place, when he gets all sentimental on me.

He says he wishes nothing but happiness for me and my girlfriend, his boss, as well. I could not help but notice he had always seemed to have a soft spot in his heart for her, so I asked him if he had ever asked her out.

To my complete surprise, he tells me he used to date her before Jim did!

Holy shit! Now I understand why he and Jim never really got along.

So, this became quite the strange working environment, one I was not completely comfortable with. We were all professional about it, but it was strange.

Funny thing was, after work, we would all have some beers at the home/office, and it was never a big issue. We all got along as if there was no past or present situation.

Eventually, Craig left for a union job to get more hours, so I became more prominent in the company. I began to learn heating and gas.

Jim and I would do private jobs for people he knew on the weekends, every so often. He had the perfect situation of doing work for the company nine to five, Monday to Friday, but serving his own customers on weekends.

I would ask questions and soon learned the paperwork and billing side of the business. It always made me wonder why Jim didn't just quit and start his own business, but he was comfortable in the situation he was in. I now know it takes a lot of drive to get over that hurdle, be self sufficient, and motivated.

I finished my last term of school in December of '94. I had been living in basement suites and my parents' place up until then, and decided it was now time to look at buying a house. I was still dating my plumbing girl and must admit, things were going well after nearly two years.

It was now the summer of '96 and I had saved up enough money, with some help from Mom and Dad, for a down payment. I was at the point where my parents thought I should be settling down and thinking of marriage, but was this what I wanted?

I decided to ask my girl if she was interested in moving in together. She said yes and we began to look at houses to take the next step in this relationship. We eventually settled on a little rancher in an area called Surrey.

It was great to finally have my own place. I actually enjoyed working on odd jobs around the house and cutting the grass. I felt I was finally coming into my own. Unfortunately, things were not going so well with the girlfriend . . . at work, or at home.

She realized her comfort zone was back at home with her mom, and I realized I still wanted to party and have my independence. I often hung out with my cousin and his friends who lived close by. I was partying with them most weekends, while she was back in her neck of the woods with her friends and family.

We decided to go our separate ways.

I now had a mortgage solely in my name. Work was slow at her company as well, and with the current situation, I cut my ties and started to look for other work.

I had been spoiled with this job; it was very casual and we all just kind of did what we wanted as long as the work got done. I answered a couple of ads in the paper, but was this want I wanted? No! I was now ready to start my own business! I had learned enough from this experience to get out there and make big money. I was now schooled in the art of heating. I had more experience in plumbing and was now fluent in gas pipe install. I was now recognized by the provincial and federal government as a journeyman plumber and class B gas fitter! The world was mine to conquer!

Or so I thought.

Chapter 12

The Birth of the Penguin

I had made up my mind. I was going to start my own business. I had saved a little money and thought this would be the perfect new start, but I needed a catchy name. I remember hearing some advertising guru say people relate well with animals or characters. Find a name people will remember, and that's half the battle. So, based on this, I ran a few names through my head. I came up with Penguin Plumbing.

Have you ever looked back on something you've done years ago and thought, "What the hell was I thinking?" This is one of those times for me.

It sounded catchy at the time, but I now see it comparable to the mullet hair cut or disco music. We know where they ended up.

I had a representative from the local Yellow Pages go over some ideas for advertising. I wanted to go big. I decided on a quarter-page ad in the big book serving the entire lower mainland. I was still driving my Ford Ranger, but I planned to turn it into a makeshift plumbing van until I could afford a real one. I assumed buying the van wouldn't take long. I would just make sure the calls were coming in, and then I would lease a brand new white service van. It would be brightly decaled with a big penguin . . . maybe even have my smiling face on the side.

The ad guy told me how many households I would be reaching—in the thousands! My only concern at that moment was how I was going to keep up with the calls. I'm sure the advertising guy was seeing big commission money at this time.

He slowly worked up to the point where he had to tell me the price. I don't remember specifically, but I remember it being close to $1300 a month. Wow! To a big corporation, that probably isn't much, but to a guy starting out with a mortgage and bills . . . that's a shitload of money! Of course, the ad guy assured me the phone would be ringing off the hook.

I started to work out what I could charge per hour, what my overhead would be, and how many calls I could do per day. It appeared I could do it as long as I remained focused and watched where my money was going.

I reluctantly agreed and told him I would have a proof of the design I wanted to his people next week. I received a copy of what the ad would look like a few days later, and it didn't look half bad . . . but the bottom line was that it was a giant penguin!

When I told my family about this endeavor, I spoke with confidence and felt I had a chance at making this work. I'm sure they knew otherwise.

The ad finally came out, and guess what? The phone wasn't ringing. I did receive a few calls, but they were mainly for quotes. I find it interesting now when I get these calls.

I have been doing the job for so many years now I can usually give a basic quote over the phone. I can visualize doing the job in my head. Back then, I figured there was no way to give a quote unless you drive out and look at the job. This ends up being a waste of your time and a drain on your pocketbook for gas, not to mention wear and tear on your vehicle.

I recall going out to quote a simple leak on a kitchen sink. My plan was to get my foot in the door and, after meeting the customer, they would surely give me the job. I went in, looked at the job, and told them this was a quick, easy fix. The customer asked me what needed to be done. To show off my competency, I explained every aspect of how to fix the leak. I then explained I had all the parts to fix it. It would be the minimum callout charge. The customer then said he would think about it and call me later.

"Why?" I asked. "I'm here now. I can have this done in about forty-five minutes. I'm giving you a great price."

He said he would think about it and call me back. As he walked me to the door and thanked me for coming, I figured it out. Kevin, you idiot, you told him how to fix the job. You explained it in full detail. Why does he need you when he can now do it himself?

I learned my first valuable lesson. I showed off my plumbing skill verbally, but did not walk out with a penny. People are funny like that. They will quite often try to get as much information as they can out of you for no charge. To be competitive, most guys in my trade give free estimates, but with gas now being $1.40 per liter at the time of this writing, I don't go very far from my hometown to do so. I can usually give an estimate over the phone. I have the experience to ask a customer a few chosen details, and then give a ballpark price. If I actually go to their home, I look at the job, chat a little, but never give details on what I plan to do. They often ask me how I'll fix it, to which I reply, "Well, if you hire me, you can watch me and ask questions."

The deadly combination of being a rookie and having a brutal name for your company, are not the ingredients for success. I actually remember getting a prank call from some guy late one Saturday night saying to me, "Is this Penguin Plumbing? Who names a company Penguin Plumbing?" I'm not kidding, it really happened.

The calls were few and far between, but some were rather interesting. It is still one of the aspects I enjoy about doing this job. There was the guy who phoned me about a constantly plugging toilet. I arrived to a screaming child at the door. "Sorry about that," he said. "That's my son. He's a bit of a handful."

I asked what he thought might be down the toilet. He explained he hadn't a clue but had plunged it many times over the past month.

"It will be fine for a few days, then plugs again," he stated.

He admitted his son was probably putting things down the toilet, but he could never catch him in the act. He proceeded to tell me he had gone through a terrible divorce and had his son every other week. It appeared to me this kid did not know the meaning of discipline. The father then showed me his brand new television. What a mess!

It had the entire front screen shattered. It looked as if it had been shot with a .22 caliber bullet, dead center. In those days, screens were still made of glass; there were no plastic or polymer screens yet. Apparently, the customer bought his kid one of those big, wooden airplanes you used to see at the local fairs. It was about four feet in diameter, with a big plastic ball at the nose of the plane. They were designed so that when you throw them, they fly directly up around in a circle behind you, and come right back to the point from which you threw it. (I think you would have to be over forty to remember them.)

Anyway, this kid decides throwing this thing in the house would be a great idea, even though he was repeatedly told not to. The father just spent big money on this TV. It had to be over forty inches and in those days, I bet it was worth close to three thousand dollars. He only had it for two days when his kid somehow threw this plane at the TV, hitting it dead centre in the middle of the glass; a perfect hit that caused the glass to shatter. I'm betting this guy drinks heavy, dealing with a kid like this!

I proceed to commence work on the toilet. I use what's known as a closet auger. It's a thick snake that actually goes through the trap of the toilet and goes below the level of the floor the toilet sits on. I also use a plunger for movement of solids and whatever may be impeding the flow of the water. I went through my usual routine, and just when I thought I had it cleared, it would plug again. I went through this procedure over four times and began to get frustrated. Sure enough, this is when the customer pops his head in to ask you, "So, what did you find?"

I usually reply with the smartass answer of, "Nothing yet but when I do, you'll be the first one I show it to."

I was stumped. How could a toilet flush fine, but then after putting toilet paper through, become plugged again? I told the customer we would have to remove the toilet and put a garden hose in the bottom end. This usually flushes out what is lodged in, or gives you access to remove anything stuck in the exit hole.

Upon taking the toilet to his backyard and filling it with full water pressure, I was able to remove a large, red delicious apple. Wow!

I'm not making this stuff up, folks. This kid had taken a few bites, then shoved the rest in the toilet and flushed. How the apple made it that far into the toilet, I'll never know. Upon removing it, I noticed four clean holes, like a big piece of Swiss cheese. These were caused by my closet auger as I attempted to rid the clog. I was coring right through the apple on every try.

As I began to shake the toilet back and forth, I could hear a rattling sound. I shoved the hose in from the other end and began to remove copious amounts of coins! I swear to God, it was like an old Vegas slot machine spitting out the winnings. One after another out came quarters, nickels, dimes. You name it, they came flying out. I'll bet there was close to five dollars lying on the grass when I was done. But wait, there's more!

I began to remove plastic Looney Tunes action figures! There was Daffy, then Bugs, and I think the Tasmanian Devil eventually fell out the ass end.

All the while, the dad just watched in amazement with the sighs and moans of a man defeated. Poor bastard! This kid was going to be the death of him!

I was eventually able to get the toilet up and running. I told him to keep my card; he was probably going to need it again soon.

I remember another customer out in the Burnaby area of the lower mainland. I had done some work on his heating system, and we got along quite well. He phoned one day with a bit of a hangover and explained his toilet was plugged in his en suite bathroom. I arrived at the call to ask what he thought might be down there. He explained he was not sure, but did mention he was not able to find his pager when he got up.

(For reference, before cell phones were as small and convenient as they are now, we used pagers—small devices that fit in the palm of your hand or clipped on your belt. They only transcribed text messages.)

I once again went through my routine, but to no avail. I had to remove the toilet from the floor bolts. I found his pager. It was sitting at the base of the toilet where the unit seals to the floor. He actually asked me if there was still a display on it. (Dumbass!) I believe I gave him that look that plainly says, "Are you fucking kidding me?"

I asked him what he did last night and if he remembered flushing his pager down the shitter. He proceeded to tell me about having a few drinks at the pub watching the game, then coming home and putting his pager on the counter of the vanity in his bathroom. So how did it make it into the toilet?

It became like the Scooby Doo mystery of the week. I was Fred, driving from call to call in the mystery machine! It ends up he had the pager on vibrate, as opposed to alarm. Someone had called in the middle of the night and set off the pager. It "buzzed" its way over to the edge of the countertop. It then had to drop straight down. The only way it could have made it into the toilet bowl was to hit the full roll of toilet paper. It did so, and landed in the toilet water, as the lid was in the open position. Quite the journey for this little pager! The customer does remember using the facilities late that night and did not have the light on. He flushed without noticing the pager at the bottom of the bowl, and there you have it—mystery solved. What are the chances of that?

I'm willing to bet a large number of people today have dropped their cell phones in a toilet. I know I have. A few too many beers at my cousin's annual get together and . . . whoopsie!

Sometimes you meet customers that are a little off center from normal. If I'm being completely honest, it's much more than "sometimes."

The cleanliness of some people's homes quite often leaves much to be desired. Upon entering a home I always wipe my boots off, although many times the soles of my boots are cleaner, with fewer bacteria, than the customer's floor.

I love it when people ask me why I don't have "booties." I sternly reply, "Because I'm a professional tradesman. I don't deliver mattresses." Ask the mattress guy if he has to wear C.S.A. approved steel toed boots.

I think it's probably every service guy's dream to knock on the door and have a good looking, barely dressed woman greet them with a smile. Then she would say something like, "Oh, I'm sorry, Mister Plumber, I was just in the shower and couldn't find a thing to wear!"

Hmm . . . Dear Penthouse, I'm a plumber, and this one day . . . Uh, sorry, where was I?

Believe me, guys in the industry talk, and we quite often have a good round of stories about situations such as these. I'm sure many of them are exaggerated, but the basis of the story is probably pretty close. I have had a few in my time, but nothing too crazy.

There was this one lady in particular who was wearing a rather low cut top on a hot summer day. It did not leave much to the imagination, if you know what I mean.

I had to work in the ceiling area in a tight spot, on a ladder. I was not able to take my tool bucket into the confined space, nor was I able to rest it on the ladder. The customer, being the sweetheart she was, offered to get the tools as I needed them from the bucket. The bucket rested on the ground, which meant she had to bend over the get the tools. Let's just say the view was stunning when she bent over to get each tool I needed.

I recall needing a lot of small, hard-to-find tools out of my bucket that day. I also recall finding as many problems to fix as possible.

I will always remember the one call that was "over the top" in this category. I rang the bell to have this beautiful woman answer the door in her underwear. No bullshit, she was wearing Calvin Klein high cut panties with a Victoria Secret-type bra!

I remember freezing in the moment, as I stuttered to introduce myself. She appeared as if she had perhaps just woken up. She said hello and walked me to the kitchen sink.

I asked what the problem was. She opened the kitchen cabinet doors to explain there was a leak under the right side. I asked her to run some water to show me. She apologized for not clearing the area under the sink and began to empty out the area.

As this goddess lay before me on her hands and knees, I had to refrain from drooling on myself. Rather than offering to help, I just kind of stood there like some child that just shit himself and isn't quite sure how to tell his mom.

She looked up at me and smiled. I can't remember if my mouth was still agape or not, but I smiled back. I then forced myself to speak and told her I was going to get a trouble light and parts.

I had to pinch myself to ensure this was real. This lady could have easily been a professional model—just beautiful. I assumed she had just got out of bed with her undergarments, so when I went back in she would probably have changed. Nope! To my pleasant surprise, she stood there with her morning coffee asking me if there was enough space under the sink. I don't remember what I mumbled back, but she asked if I wanted a coffee. Like a nervous kid, I replied, "No thanks. I'm trying to quit."

Was this my attempt at trying to be funny? What an idiot! Stick to plumbing, Kev. Leave the jokes to the professionals! She smiled and went upstairs.

I continued my work on the sink. I could not help but notice she was now going up and down the stairs with laundry, still dressed in the underwear. So now I'm thinking, *Alright, she's single and she's hinting that she wants me.*

This is it, Kev. The good Lord is giving you a gift for all your hard work. When opportunity knocks, make sure you open the door.

I checked the armpits of my shirt to make sure I smelled fresh. I checked my hair in the reflection of the glass doors. I decided I would start a conversation when she came back into the room.

I wheeled around to find a rather big dude enter the kitchen in his bathrobe. He grabbed a coffee and said good morning. I acknowledged his presence and felt disappointment. Yup, too good to be true. She was married. But wait, this gets better.

By the time the job was done, they were both chatting with me about whatever. They seemed like a nice couple. Somehow, they started talking about their cabin in the woods. I can't remember where it was, but I stated I loved the wilderness, fishing, and camping. They said I should come up and party with them sometime.

People always say this to be polite, so I said, "Sure."

It was mentioned a new fridge for their kitchen was just purchased; they needed the water line run for the ice maker. I was asked if this is a job I could do. I said yes, but told them I did not have the parts with me. I would pick them up and come back tomorrow night.

That would be a Sunday night, but I was desperate for business and trying to build a clientele. Whatever it takes! I left there thinking something was a little strange about those two. It would not have surprised me if they took me downstairs to show me some kind of film studio where they shot their own porn movies—not really creepy, just kinda different.

I returned the next night to hook up the water line for the fridge. The two were in the middle of what appeared to be the tail end of a romantic dinner. By the time I finished the job, they were enjoying another glass of wine and asking me to join them.

What? How awkward would that be? I politely declined, but they insisted I have a drink with them. I love my beer, so asked if they had any.

I sat down and enjoyed polite conversation with them; that is until they started talking about the cabin in the woods. Then, they asked if I wanted to go up with them. This was no longer polite etiquette; they were serious. Just the three of us, together at their cabin. What the hell had I gotten myself into?

I figured it was one of three things:

1. He wanted to watch as I had fun with his wife.
2. They wanted a threesome.
3. They wanted to drag me out to the woods and bury me behind the woodshed!

Although I briefly entertained the thought of the first one, I was not about to roll the dice and find out it was the last one. I thanked them for the drink and politely made my way out the door.

Maybe I over-analyzed the situation, but you be the judge. The whole experience just had "strange" written all over it.

Financially, things were starting to get tough. I had to cancel the Yellow Pages ad, which meant I lost my main phone line for the business. How were customers going to get a hold of me now?

I needed a roommate to help me with the bills.

I had this one clown move in. Strange guy that could not seem to hold a job. He soon left. I put an ad in the paper again, and I had this very polite Korean fellow knock at the door. I thought maybe he was selling something and was surprised when he said his name was George. I had spoken to him on the phone, but his English was well versed; I did not realize he was Korean.

It ends up he was a radiologist in his home country, but was not recognized as one here in Canada. Different qualifications are needed. He was taking courses to upgrade himself, and then attempting to get a job. His wife and family were back in Korea. He often phoned them, and they would fly in to see him every other month.

George moved in and was a good man. I often felt bad, as it was now winter and I kept the temperature of the house very low to save money. He was rather thin, and was probably freezing his little Korean ass off. I opened the door to his room one day to find a multitude of electric heaters in his room. Poor guy.

I lived off Kraft dinners and Ramen noodles. The only good meals I had were when Mom and Dad invited me over for Sunday dinner. I was also starting to get skinny. I was miserable, lonely, and broke. Funny thing was I was still trying to figure out ways to improve the business and change things. But the reality was, I was broke and in debt to my bills, I was lonely, and I had to look at myself in the mirror and admit I had failed.

The next day, I was cutting my lawn and my neighbor asked how things were going. I was honest and told him the truth. He said he had noticed my truck was not out of the driveway much, which meant I probably wasn't working.

He mentioned to me his brother-in-law was the foreman of a big job site just outside of town. He was looking to hire journeyman plumbers.

My neighbor had already put a good word in for me, so I high tailed it out to the job site and introduced myself. We chatted. He asked me about my business. It turns out he was not looking to hire an employee, but wanted to hire a subcontractor to work with him. He asked what my business charged per hour, and it appeared to fit his budget. It looked like I had the job!

At the end of the day, I was shocked at how things can turn around in the course of twenty-four hours.

Chapter 13

Out of the Frying Pan, Into the Fire

When a company is hired to do a job, they sometimes have aspects of the job they don't really handle, or there is too much work for the amount of manpower they have. So, rather than hire employees for that small job, they hire another company to come in and help them out. This is known as "subcontracting."

The benefits to this would be that the company hired has all their own insurance coverage, tools, and is self sufficient with their own transportation.

It was a situation that seemed perfect for me at the time. Rather than closing my company name—as shitty as it was—and having to go back to being an employee, I was now still my own company and getting paid that way. I was essentially working under his permits and doing what he wanted, but the pay was much better than being an employee. Plus, I still had all my write-offs.

The project was the biggest I had ever worked on. The job site was an entire city block. It was to be a hotel, with a nightclub and a restaurant attached at both ends. Wow! There must have been close to fifty guys at all times on that site. Always busy.

I learned quite a bit. We were putting in all the underground services, like the water mains and all the drain lines out to the city. I met a lot of great guys and got to know most of the excavating crew.

We had this old guy working the bulldozer and backhoe. This guy was a genius with that machine. One day, he had one of the young apprentices light their cigarette and stand in the ditch.

We all watched in amazement as this old guy brought this huge digging bucket forward, and slowly proceeded to flick the ash off the end of the smoke. That takes years of talent, folks!

I also became pretty tight with the supervisor of the entire site. He was this little skinny guy named Ted. He was the type of guy you would normally see pushing a pencil in an office somewhere. This guy did not appear to have any knowledge of how to run a job of this magnitude. He looked like he would be a good candidate for the TV show, *Canada's Worst Handyman.*

We got to talking one day and I found out I wasn't too far off. This was his first big project. He was a little nervous but was taking it one day at a time. I admired that. Taking on a job of this size would have scared most guys away. But, he was sick of his old job and wanted a new career in life. Talk about jumping in with both feet! I soon found out he would not be the only one taking that jump.

It became rather evident that Ted and my contractor were not seeing eye to eye. I think it was over money, or who was making the final decisions on whatever. To my surprise, I showed up one day to find out my contractor had quit. This was my neighbor's brother-in-law, so when I arrived home I wanted to find out what the hell was going on.

Turns out he told Ted to go fuck himself, packed up his tools, and headed back to Alberta. They had an argument about something, and that was the last straw. Did I still have a job to go to? Who was going to run the show?

This all happened on a Friday, so when I arrived at work on the Monday, Ted pulls me into his office. At this time, all of the underground plumbing had been done. There were still water lines and drain lines inside the buildings to complete.

One of the guys I worked with, Dave, was a very knowledgeable plumber, but did not have his journeyman ticket. He had actually run a few jobs on his own, but because he was not adept at math he was never able to pass the government exam. Turns out he was going to complete all the plumbing. His brother-in-law actually worked on the site as the sprinkler fitter. Because he had his own company, the brother-in-law took over the permits and allowed Dave to run the plumbing show. But now the gas lines had to be run for all buildings. Who was going to take on that huge job? Enter the Penguin!

Ted asked if I had my gas ticket. I said yes. He then explained he needed someone to run all the piping for the job site. This was to be a huge job. I had my ticket, but passing a test on paper and actually doing a large job were two different things. Normally, a guy would start off small, like doing a house, for instance. I was about to take on an entire hotel complex with a restaurant and night club. I hesitated and told him I had never done a job of this magnitude. Ted explained he did not have the time to look for another contractor. They were behind schedule and needed someone to start NOW! Then we started talking money.

I honestly don't remember what he offered me per hour, but it was more money than I had ever made. If I were to take this on, I could look my family in the eye and feel I wasn't a failure. It would mean the idea of starting my own business would be a successful endeavor, not a stupid decision made by a confused, cocky kid. It would also mean I could start paying my bills and get out of debt.

What was I going to do if I did not take this job? Go back to working for someone else? I had too much pride for that. I started thinking about that guy at the airport job who said I would never make it. I heard the voice of my father who was always telling me to get back to the grind and do it the old fashioned way. Stop this running your own business idea.

If I didn't take this opportunity, I would always wonder where it could have led me. Why I was a coward, and didn't bother trying. I did not possess the experience or knowledge to complete even a job half this size, but I looked Ted in the eye and said YES!

I had to now get an insurance bond for the company and a business license for the city I was working in. Ted's people paid for all that. I then pulled all the permits. I was ready to go, but didn't have a clue where to start.

I remember reading the code book every night trying to get myself up to speed. I didn't even own a proper threading machine for the iron gas pipe. I had an old manual threader my uncle had given me. I rented a chain vise to hold the pipe and had an old squirt bottle to apply oil to the cutting reamer. Talk about low budget. Guys on the job site were looking at me and shaking their heads. I can only imagine what they must have thought.

I hired my cousin Murray to come out and give me a hand. He was laid off at the time, so I paid him cash at the end of the day. I had never used this manual threader before, so gave Murray a basic briefing on how to use it. He came back a half hour later and told me it just wasn't working. I went over to try it myself and realized I had the threading head in backwards! Holy shit! What had I got myself into? My first day on the site and I can't even work my own tools properly.

It got worse. I had Murray start digging trenches so I could lay my underground gas pipe. The pipe I ordered did not arrive when scheduled, so all the trenches Murray dug were left exposed to the weather. The area was mainly sand, and on the morning of my pipe arriving, it was a torrential downpour of rain. I arrived at the job site to see all Murray's hard work gone.

All the trenches had caved in. It took two days to dig them back out. I was getting close to calling it quits; nothing seemed to be going right.

Murray was soon back to work at his regular job and I was on my own. This allowed me to concentrate more on my task at hand, rather than always trying to keep my employee busy. Once I learned to calm down and stop feeling sorry for myself, I noticed the job starting to take form. I soon had all the underground lines run and tested. I was now finishing up the lines for the nightclub and was about to start the hotel.

The city inspector was a great guy, which made things go smoothly as well. He knew I was pretty "green," so he was very patient with me. I asked a lot of questions and he always took the time to answer them.

Before I knew it, the summer was coming to an end and I was nearing the end of the project. I passed all my inspections and was quite proud when looking back at what I had accomplished. I never would have thought I could have done it on my own, but I did, and it was the best thing I could have done.

I do remember the gas inspector saying to me, "Next time, you might want to have a little more experience when you take on a job this size." To which I replied, "Well, ya

gotta start somewhere."

I accomplished this huge job with a pick, shovel, and an old manual pipe threader from the sixties. I worked from the back of a pickup truck and had a bucket for a toolbox. I had many strange looks from other contractors, but I didn't care, I DID IT!

Ted had mentioned they were starting another project early the next year, so I asked if they wanted me to be the plumbing and gas contractor. He said we would discuss it when the time came closer. I figured now that I had done one, I would have an easier time with the next. So now I had a decision to make. Do I wait until the next big project starts? Or do I go back to working as an employee at another plumbing and heating company?

I no longer had advertising to do my service work, because I knew that avenue was not going to pay the bills. I had now worked my way out of debt; I certainly wasn't going to go back into it.

Riding the high of completing this big job, I decided to wait until the new project started in the spring. But what was I going to do in the meantime for work? I was not able to claim employment insurance benefits, as they are not an option when you run your own company.

One of my good friends at the time was manager of the home audio department at a company called A & B Sound.

At one time, they were the popular outlet for buying CD's, DVD's, car and home audio etc. Long before the big companies of today like Future Shop and Best Buy.

We got chatting one night and I told him of my situation. I needed a job to get me by until the spring. He tells me the holiday season is one of their busiest times. He then told me the money he makes on his commissions. Wow! Those guys can do pretty well financially when the business is good. He said I should come and work with him. What? Me doing sales at A & B Sound? He said after I learned the product lines, the rest was easy. I was single at the time, and he said it was a great way to meet women. Hmm . . . that sounded intriguing.

I would be selling VCRs, TVs, CD players, and camcorders. I knew how all those things worked, and I had the "gift of the gab," as some would put it. After taking the weekend to think about it, I kind of relished the idea of just getting out of the trade for a while. No more wearing overalls and jeans; I would now be wearing a suit and tie to work, again!

I thought to myself, *How difficult could it be?* After all, if I could install gas pipe in a hotel complex, this should be like taking candy from a baby! I called Terry and told him I would be there for Monday morning. He laughed and said, "Awesome, buddy. You're gonna love it here."

Chapter 14

Life in Retail Sales

I am going to start this chapter by saying I have the utmost respect for anyone who works in retail sales.

There are so many different approaches people use when wanting to buy a product. Some already know what they want, know the approximate price, and, as long as you are in that ballpark, they easily buy the product. Other people, well, let's just say it might be easier to solve world peace before giving them what they expect.

I showed up Monday as promised and met the guys I would be working with. Most construction guys you meet have a pretty good physical build on them, with leathery hands from years of physical labor. I found it strange to see these skinny guys with hands smoother than a woman's, looking like they had never seen the inside of a gym. They were all nicely dressed, nice haircuts, and some wearing cologne. Wow! This was going to be a different world for me.

They whisked me into a back room where I was shown a few videos on how to best approach people. How to listen to what the customer wants, as opposed to what you want them to know. I especially found it valuable when they taught the tips on how to close a deal that is getting close, or when a customer appears inclined to walk away. I still remember these teachings and sometimes they come in handy when I'm quoting a big job. One does not want to seem desperate, but if you know the product you are selling, and make the customer feel they are making the best decision for their family and budget, you will quite often make the sale.

It should be mentioned that most retail electronic sales, in that day, were all commission sales. If you wanted to purchase an item, you had to go through a sales representative to do so, much like buying furniture. (Now, you just grab what you want off the shelves; salespeople are there only if you ask for their assistance.)

The hardest part was learning the product lines, which ones were the top end and which were crap. It was also important to learn the product lines that paid you the most commission. Often, a salesperson will fill you in on the information of the product you came in to buy, but they are also professionally trained to show and convince you that another product line is twice as good for just a little more money. That's how they make better commission.

Many product lines are household names that people know. They advertise them heavily, but will always try to push you to another brand that pays more commission. If you have to go through a salesman to purchase something, I can assure you this is almost always the case.

I recall a time when this young couple came in looking to buy a new TV. All of us working would take turns as to who was able to approach the next customer, and it was my turn. Our displays of televisions were stacked three high on three separate shelves, each running about thirty feet long. The upper shelf was a little on the high side, and was sometimes difficult to get to when the need arose to show its capabilities.

As usual, most customers want a well-known brand name, like Sony. I remember showing them the latest model, but did so with a complete lack of enthusiasm. The reason was not that Sony made a bad TV; on the contrary, Sony has always made one of the best televisions on the market. I knew the JVC model had a better warranty, and that I would make more commission if I sold it.

I proceeded to the top level of televisions to give my well-rehearsed speech on the benefits of this fine machine. Now, keep in mind, this was many years ago when there was no such thing as flat screens, plasmas, or LCDs. All these units were big, bulky, and heavy, with glass screens and the protruding back ends as deep as the TV was wide. I would say the average size on the display rack was thirty-two inches and weighed about a hundred and forty pounds.

The customer and his wife seemed to be very interested in my vast knowledge of this unit. Things were going great, until he asked me how many inputs/outputs it had in the back for extra jacks. Well, I proceeded to turn the television around to show him the back end and see for myself. The damn thing was already on an angle and I was pushing my luck in even moving it slightly. I was sure I had the majority of the weight balanced to the middle, but unfortunately, I did not. As I began to point out the input jacks, the last thing I heard was, "LOOK OUT!"

I had moved the television too close to the edge of the shelf. SMASH!

The damn thing fell from the top shelf and came crashing to the ground. Pieces of shattered plastic and glass lay in a pile at my feet. Fortunately, no one was hurt.

The entire store went absolutely silent. All eyes were focused on me, mouths agape as they tentatively waited to see me crumble. Without missing a beat, I looked at my customers and said, "You know, we have a great deal on a little unit over here in the corner."

The surrounding customers burst into laughter, and I got a few pats on the back from fellow employees for handling the situation so well. And yes, the young couple did buy the TV!

I had the chance to meet some great coworkers, a few I still keep in touch with today. I was often asked what store I worked at before this one. When I told them I was a licensed plumber and had just finished a big gas job for my own small company, they looked at me as if I was nuts.

They would often ask, "You're a licensed tradesman and you're working here?" I would explain the circumstances that led me there and explained I did not think this was going to be a permanent gig.

The hours there were not always easy going and fun. It's obviously pretty busy and stressful when there is a big sale, or around Christmas time.

I recall selling an item to a woman who appeared to be of Asian descent. I was in a hurry, as I had other customers waiting to see me. Because of cramped space at the store, most things were on display, and then the customer would go to the lower floor to pick the item up at the warehouse area.

It was my job to give the cashier on the main floor the purchase order, and then another copy to the shipper/receiver. The customer told me she was going to shop for a few compact discs while I distributed my paperwork. My cashier asked who the paperwork belonged to, so she could get her to sign for it after it was processed. I was in a hurry and did not think to be politically correct. I casually pointed in her direction and said, "It's the Chinese lady in the blue shirt."

Next day, I was pulled into the general manager's office and told to close the door.

Apparently, the woman was from the Philippines and took offense to me calling her Chinese. So much so she called up the store to complain about me. Yikes! I learned very quickly to be careful what you say about people's ethnicity. It's hard these days, because the politically correct terms for people of different countries and origins are constantly changing. I remember being a kid and hearing adults at parties making jokes about other races and religions. That shit doesn't fly today, and people are very sensitive when it comes to humor.

I often used to try to break the ice with a customer by telling a funny story or a joke. I tend not to do that anymore as it is so easy to get yourself in trouble by offending someone. Ah, how the times have changed!

I remember getting pulled aside by this same manager one day. It was great when decisions concerned our department because my buddy Terry was the boss. But anything in another department was not. This guy was fat and kind of quiet. I didn't really like him and I kind of made that known to him. He knew most people would kiss his ass because they wanted to get up the sales ladder. Me, I knew this was a temporary gig for a few months. I was just waiting for him to try and push me around. That day was here.

He tells me they have had painters in at night to spice up the car audio area a little. They had been cleaning their brushes and rollers off in the utility sink in the back room. The lines were plugged and the sink needed repairs. "You're a plumber, I hear. Go and take a look at that, and see if you can fix it."

I looked at him with a slight smile on my face.

"Sure," I said. "I have next Monday off, so I'll come in with my tools and see what I can do. Do you want a quote for my hourly rate?"

This asshole shakes his head at me and states that he wants it looked at now, and I'll be doing it for my current rate at work. The problem with this is most salesmen make minimum wage as an hourly rate; they make their living on commissions of what they sell. If my head is under a sink, I can't sell merchandise. This was a losing proposition for me, and I explained that to his fat face. I don't remember all the details but suffice to say; I got the "You're the new guy" speech and "You get all the shit jobs if you want to keep working here." It was about this point I decided it was time to pull the plug on this job.

I went to speak to Terry, as I could not believe what I was being asked to do. Terry said he would have a chat with him as soon as he had a chance. In Terry's opinion, the manager was probably not serious, and perhaps I took it wrong. He asked if maybe I could just take a quick look at it to assess what needed to be done; maybe take a shot at it with a plunger.

Rather than telling everybody where they could shove the plunger, I decided to just do what was asked to end this circus

110

on a good note. I think I did get the water to drain, but that was about it.

I called Terry that weekend to thank him for the opportunity, and that it had been fun. He understood and wished me well.

I now had no doubt in my mind. It was time to get back to what I knew. Working retail sales gave me a much-needed appreciation for my trade, and I now had the desire to get back to it.

Chapter 15

Back to the Grind

I started making phone calls to the old group I worked for on the big hotel gas job. They were starting to set up shop at the new site, so I went out to give them a visit and maybe set the ground work for getting myself back in.

I spoke to Ted and did not get a good vibe. It was the kind of attitude you give somebody on the phone when you really don't want to talk anymore. Upon leaving, it became quite clear I was not in their plans for the next big project.

I realized I was a last minute fill-in on the last job, but I was under the impression I had done great and was slated to be their new contractor.

Truth is, when I look back now, I was still very inexperienced and green. I really didn't have the manpower or knowledge to complete a job this big from start to finish. I did not want to admit that then, but I sure will now. Sometimes things happen for a reason. I have found that expression to be very true.

I swallowed my pride and knew I had to get back to work doing the nine to five grind, working for someone else. I answered an ad in the paper for a plumbing/heating/gas company in the White Rock area of town. For legal reasons, I'll change the name slightly and call them Energy-Save.

They had about five technicians on the road, and the boss would do the occasional call as well.

He was a big, heavy-set guy, and he and I hit it off as my interview went quite well. He called me back the next week to start my new job.

I soon met the group and had the pleasure of knowing two of the best troubleshooting technicians I have ever met, Roger and Rob. They were almost polar opposites and at different stages of life, but I learned many things, along with many beers and laughs.

Rob was one of the most easygoing guys you would ever want to meet. Honestly, this guy would give you the shirt off his back or his last dollar if you really needed it. He had a heart of gold. Unfortunately, he had an ex-wife who had really taken advantage of that and had really done him in.

I think at this time she was living out of town with their three kids, and he was stuck paying most of the bills. He would see the kids once a month or so and always looked forward to seeing them when it was his weekend. If I remember correctly, his ex's parents were lawyers or something, so we can all figure out who got shafted in that divorce! I would always feel somewhat sorry for him, but he never cried the pity tears or expected anyone to feel bad for him.

The one thing his divorce did leave him with, however, was a bit of a drinking problem. Rob loved his beers. Now don't get me wrong, I love my beers, too, but not so much on a weeknight when you have to go to work the next morning. He was not a big guy, but, man, he sure could put 'em back. He would go through a case like it was water. He was never arrogant or belligerent; he was just one of those kind souls that got happier as he drank.

I would often ride with him, as we would be paired together for larger projects. Many of the tools and tricks of the trade I use to this day, I learned from him.

One day I said good morning to him, and I could just see he was still piss drunk from the night before. His eyes were like two piss holes in the snow, as the expression goes. When I got in the van with him, the vehicle smelled like a brewery. Partially from the booze on his breath, and partially from the twenty or so empties piled in the back.

"Holy shit dude, you're a mess!" I told him.

"Ya," he said. "Maybe you should drive."

Fortunately, the first call of the morning was not far from the shop. The customer was an old lady, and we were told to just go downstairs and fix the furnace.

"Come up if you need anything," she said.

I felt like asking her to put on a pot of strong coffee for beer boy, but did not want to impose.

First thing I did was shove a breath mint into him. Not just for the customer's sake, but for mine as well, since I was getting a buzz off the fumes. I had a basic knowledge of trouble shooting, but Rob still held my hand in most cases.

He told me to see if I could figure this one out, as his eyes were half closed. I asked him questions while I checked all aspects of the system. I finally diagnosed the fact that the furnace needed a new gas valve. We did not have the type needed in the van, so I told him to hold tight while I drove back to the office to get one.

To set the scene in this old basement, the elderly lady obviously had old stuff stored there for years. Pictures on the wall would indicate that her husband had probably passed away a few years ago, and her kids seemed to be using the basement as their personal storage locker. There was an old foldout army cot in one corner. The thing was covered in cobwebs and probably hadn't been used in years.

I returned with a large cup of Tim Horton's coffee for Rob, and the gas valve required, but where was Rob? I followed the smell of beer and the sound of snoring to find him sleeping soundly on the old cot. You had to see it. His hair and shirt were full of cobwebs and he had found a pink baby's blanket to wrap around him that said, "I love Grandma." Priceless!

We did not have cameras on our phones in those days, but what a time for a picture. I let him sleep as I changed the gas valve. About an hour later, I woke sleeping beauty to give him his now cold coffee and tell him it was time to pack up.

"Did you get the gas valve?" he asked.

"Yes, it's already installed and I fired the furnace; it's done."

He had that stunned look as he asked, "Wow, how long have I been out?"

I told him to tuck his shirt in and clean off the cobwebs, as we were on to the next call.

The amazing thing is, we actually went to the pub after work, and he picked up right where he left off.

Then there was Roger. I was never really able to put my finger on whether this guy was as good as he claimed to be, or just a great bullshitter. Even years later as I write this, I am chuckling to myself because I still don't know.

Roger was a great guy as well, and if he liked you, you were in. He would be very loyal to his friends and quiet to those he was not sure of. He was married with a daughter and lived fairly close to where I lived. We both shared a passion for fishing and, let me tell you, this guy could fish. He had some native blood in his background, and he would be the only one catching fish on the lake or river when no one else could.

I'm not kidding. He took me river fishing one day for steelhead. He always knew the best places to go. I remember one day he put on his polarized glasses and told me to look at this little back eddy swirl across the river.

"Do you see that one?" he asked.

"Uh . . . see what?" I said.

"Right there, in that little pool."

I honestly squinted for about half a minute to see nothing. I figured he was full of shit and just trying to impress me. I was going to call him out and suggest he cast into it to catch this mystery fish. Well, I did not have to call him out, as he reared back his line and tossed it towards the pool.

I watched him make about four casts and, I shit you not, he nailed it! His rod tip went nuts and he began to fight what was probably a fifteen-pounder. He never did bring it in, but the proof was there.

I had always found river fishing to be a bit stressful, as one is often competing for spots on the river with other anglers. I prefer the calm and serenity of fishing a lake in a boat or off the shore. I have many fond memories of my dad taking me as a kid to his favorite lake in the B.C. Interior. We would rent a cabin and fish for days in a little twelve-foot aluminum boat.

I love being out on the water. I had always wanted to learn to fly fish as well. I mentioned this to Roger, and a big smile came across his face.

It was not long after that Roger and I were hang'n out all the time. We would often meet early on Saturday mornings and go out fishing for the day. He taught me what to look for in a fly rod, and I soon had one. I then purchased something called a Belly-Boat. It's basically a glorified inner-tube you would use as a kid to float down the local stream or in a pool. It has strapping in the middle so you can sit in it. You put on a set of scuba coveralls called neoprenes, as this protects you from the cold water. For just over a hundred bucks, viola! You're out on the water fly-fishing.

Roger was even better at trouble shooting problems with forced air heating, hydronics, plumbing, and pumps. You name it and this guy was able to figure it out. Because he and I were hang'n out so much, I would often stop by his place after work for a couple of beers. He's the only guy I know that likes to drink his beer warm. Weird!

We would sit down and he would ask me if I had any questions about what we did that day.

One evening, I remember him taking apart his thermostats and drawing me a diagram on how the low voltage systems work on boilers and furnaces. He had patience and a wealth of knowledge to share. I don't recall him having a lot of close friends in his inner circle, but I felt privileged he called me one of them.

It was not long until the boss gave me my own van. This was a pretty big confidence move for any employer. It shows your job is pretty secure and that he trusts you. If he did not feel you had potential to make him money, he would not take that step with you. But in this case, I was doing well and really liked my new position.

All was going well the first few days with the van, until I realized that doing maintenance on this beast had not been a priority. I was travelling at a pretty good clip when the car in front of me hit the brakes for an upcoming construction area. It was poorly marked, as you barely had time to react driving around the corner. I applied the brakes but there was not a whole bunch of stopping going on. BAM!

No one was hurt, just my pride and a couple of bent fenders. I drove back to the shop and told of my incident. I felt like giving them shit for not fixing the brakes, but thought it better to keep my mouth shut and offer to pay the deductable from my check. They, of course, agreed that was a swell idea. I didn't want to rock the boat, as I was doing well here and liked it.

My luck did not get any better, as a few weeks later, Roger and I were soldering pipes in the mechanical room of a large apartment building full of seniors. I should be more accurate by saying he was doing the pipe fitting, and I commenced soldering.

Upon doing so, I forgot to check for smoke detectors. Most commercial buildings have heat detectors—they go off like a sprinkler head under extreme heat—and smoke does not affect them.

Well, just my luck, I get an old building with smoke detectors and off they go, as I am just getting into my fourth solder joint. It would not have been so bad if it was just alarming that room, but as I stepped out into the parking garage, alarm bells were ringing throughout the entire building. My only thought was, *OH SHIT!*

This meant every senior in a wheelchair or walker had to exit the building. I looked at Roger. He had his head in his hands and was suppressing his laughter. All I could come up with was to look at him and say, "Whoopsie daisies."

He walked by me and said he would find the manager and explain what happened, while I stayed in the parking garage. To my dismay the situation got worse, as Roger came back to tell me the alarms were directly linked to the local fire department!

I no sooner receive the news than, seconds later, the sirens could be heard coming down the block.

Two fire trucks arrived and what seemed like an army of firefighters started walking through the parking garage doors.

I'll never forget Roger just walking over to his van and casually sitting on his front bumper, as if to say, "You're on your own, kid. I'm not saying a word."

I could feel the nervous tension build as these firemen in all their gear walked up to me. It was like a scene from that Kurt Russell movie, *Backdraft*.

I believe I have mentioned before my smart-ass mouth sometimes gets me in trouble, and this was one of those times. I did not want to show any guilt or weakness, so decided to come up with a wisecrack to break the tension. The fire captain stood in front of me, and I smiled and said, "I was soldering and forgot to cover the alarms. Sorry for interrupting your card game at the station!"

If the fire captain could have stuck a hose up my ass, I think he would have. What a stupid thing to say on my part. Roger, once again, was shaking his head in that disapproving way only a father can do when you tell him you wrecked the family car.

Don't get me wrong. I chuckle when I think about it now, but at the time . . . yikes!

I received a stern talking to about fire safety from the chief, and I promised it would not happen again. Nowadays, they charge you if they come out on a false alarm. You have to check with the building manager to see if there are any detectors and, if so, they are to make a call to the local fire department telling them of a possible call. Should a false alarm come in, the fire department will have a contact number to the building and confirm before they come out.

I guess it's the law of averages, or just the law of physics, which states all that goes up, must come down.

I was moving up the ranks at the company and doing well, only to make a bad decision that eventually ended in disaster.

Just prior to starting with Energy-Save, I had tried selling my subcontracting services to a few companies, hoping I could survive on jobs they couldn't handle. It obviously didn't pan out, but I did meet a front desk girl I eventually started dating. We ended up moving in together.

She did not drive, and the commute to her job was now too far. It just so happened that our current front office girl was going to have a baby and would soon be going on maternity leave. They needed someone to replace her.

Well, it just made sense to me to get my girlfriend the job. This was exactly what she had been doing, and now we could car pool to work. Sounds great, right? Wrong!

There is definitely a reason why people warn against spouses working with each other and/or dating someone from the office. It rarely works out. I, unfortunately, had to learn this the hard way. My girlfriend ended up getting the job and soon me, her, Rob, and Roger were all hanging out like one big happy family. This whole thing seemed to fit so naturally.

I was feeling good about my future. I assume it was for this reason I proposed to this girl. She said yes, and I thought this would be a fairytale ending. Looking back now, there was most certainly an ending, but no fairytale here, folks!

The norm in the office was that the service calls would be put on the bulletin board the night before. Roger was the senior technician, so he would have first choice. Rob would have second choice, and I would get what was left. My now fiancée had a great idea to save the company money on gas and wear and tear on the vehicles. She would group the calls into sequence according to their locations, so therefore techs would not be driving erratically all over the city.

This idea, on paper, was great and the boss loved her thinking. The idea was implemented.

Unfortunately, this tended to remove Roger from having his choice, thus somewhat removing his seniority. I must admit I started getting the cushier jobs and was no longer at the bottom of the list. Roger and my fiancée started to grow resentful of one another, and soon there was a problem.

I would drive home and hear nothing but complaints about Roger and his "whining." Rob had other issues to deal with, so he really didn't care either way. It was now a bit of a conflict at home whenever I mentioned I was going for beers or fishing with Roger.

I would always get the "What do you want to hang out with that pain in the ass for?" Roger began to call me less and less. What was I supposed to do? Most guys in my situation would try and keep the peace with their ladies—I think—so I just let the friendship with Roger fade.

As a couple, we then started hanging out with Rob. He was into the online dating scene, and he soon hooked up with this girl from Australia. She was a ball of energy who loved to party, and the four of us hit it off. We would often hang out on weekends and go for drinks. This soon turned into Rob and me doing jobs together, as my girl was in control of what technician went to what job.

I could sense Roger was feeling the man left out, and he soon became rather quiet to me at work. I will say nothing bad about Roger in these writings because I feel he had every right to act as he did. I probably would have done the same. I now realize most of the jobs Rob and I did together, Roger and him probably used to do.

Things began to get slow as the summer approached and people started their holidays. Now, things get not only personal, but financial as well.

Rob and I were getting most of the hours, and Roger was now the low man. I'm pretty sure Roger had a talk with the boss, as there was a change in the way the calls were distributed. You could feel the tension building, week by week, and our boss soon pulled me into the office.

My girl had a problem with getting ready in the mornings. Let's just say she was not a morning person. Since we drove to work together, it was starting to make me late for work as well. I was told to "pull up my socks," as the older generation put it, and start showing up on time. There were a few other things mentioned that were definite hints, leading me to believe he and his wife—both owners of the company—were not too happy with the way my fiancée was running the front desk. I guess they figured it was easier to get me to tell her as opposed to doing it themselves. Cowards!

Upon arriving home that night, I explained we would have to get up earlier so we could get into work sooner. This turned into a fight, and she refused to start one minute sooner than she was getting paid to.

I was now officially between a rock and a hard place; keep things happy at home, or dump the girl I had recently proposed to and keep my job. I once again took the road of having peace where I live, but should have realized that perhaps this "soon-to-be" marriage was not going to work.

We had been told very clearly by the boss doing side jobs were not permitted while we were employed with his company. This became a bone of contention, because I have always felt what a person does on his or her own time is their business.

Because I am now an owner of a company, I completely understand not wanting an employee to be using my van, my gas, my tools, and my parts to be making money for their pockets. I would consider that stealing, but I would have no problems if they use their own truck, tools, and parts. There is enough work out there for everybody, and if a guy lands a job through his own contacts, friends, or family, then I see no issues with him doing so.

We were told any job offered to us should be passed on to the company, since, in the owner's mind, it was his company that paid our bills.

Needless to say, the cohesive unit at the shop was starting to fall apart, and I think it was inevitable a change had to happen. But where would the axe fall?

It was at this time my in-laws to be had a small fire in their home. It was determined an iron had been left on and somehow fallen off the ironing board. No one was home at the time, so it eventually caught fire on the linoleum floor.

The fire took out the upper kitchen area and part of two bedrooms before the fire crews could arrive. Once the insurance issues were settled, I was asked if I was interested in doing the repairs to the plumbing, heating, and gas for rebuilding the gutted section of the home.

I, of course, said yes. There were a few areas I was not completely confident in handling and needed a hand. It just made sense to ask Rob to help me. He agreed and we decided we would tackle the job over a couple of weekends. I had my pickup truck to still do odd plumbing jobs, and still had plumbing accounts at the local wholesalers.

Unfortunately, Rob only had the Energy-Save work van as transportation, as his financial situation after the divorce had left him living paycheck to paycheck.

This would now mean both of us were breaking the rules of our employer, especially Rob, as he would be using the company van and tools to do the job. I asked him if he was comfortable with this, and he agreed.

I was using my own truck and tools. My own parts purchased under my own company name. I, therefore, felt no guilt in what I was doing; besides, it was a job for future family.

The first weekend went fine. We knew we could finish off by next weekend if we put in two good days of work. I remember telling Rob to keep this work between him and me, and not to say anything at the office. But Rob loved to talk, and I remember overhearing him talk to Roger about this whole thing.

I did not want to give him shit, but when I approached him on it, he stated, "Don't worry about Roger, he's cool. He doesn't care."

I wish I could have believed that, but now the door was open for Roger to have me fired. Even though I was using all my own stuff, I was still violating company policy by doing a side job. This whole situation was not conducive to having a good night's sleep!

But, what was I worried about? Roger and I were buddies . . . fishing buddies at that! He wouldn't rat me out, would he?

Rob and I finished the job by Sunday afternoon of the next weekend. We kicked back that evening with a few beers and a couple of steaks on the barbecue. But, we had quite the shock when we arrived at work Monday morning.

Chapter 16

The Lord Giveth, and the Lord Taketh Away

At this time, my fiancée had taken a few days off to help her parents with getting the move organized from the rental home back into their residence. So it was just Rob and I who got hauled into the office that morning. It was almost surreal, as all the other technicians left for their calls, but we were told not to go out that morning. It was like being a kid who gets called into the principal's office while all the other kids are having fun on the playground.

Rob was called in first. I waited anxiously, wondering what was going on, but knew full well what it was really about. He was probably in there for about fifteen minutes, but it seemed like hours.

He eventually came out with his always pleasant smile that kind of said, "Ah, whatever."

This was his attitude to most things in life anyway. The look on the boss's face was quite different, however, when he called me in. I knew I was not being called in for a raise or promotion.

I could not believe what I saw spread out on his desk, a full array of pictures of Rob and me working in and around the job site. There were multiple pictures of him and me carrying materials into the house. A picture of Rob pulling pipe out of the work van could clearly be seen. Another was of me stepping into the back of Rob's van to get parts. Various pictures of him and me going in and out of the home, carrying tools and plumbing parts, were strewn about the desk.

I knew the boss wasn't in the area that day to take the pictures—I would often check to see—so he must have hired a private company to follow Rob out to the job site. This was something right out of the movies!

They went through a lot of time, effort, and money to catch us in the act. I didn't realize things had gotten to that point of frustration for them. I understand firing me, but Rob was one of their best technicians; this really had nothing to do with him.

It must have taken me a minute or two to pick my jaw up off the ground, as he had me quite taken aback. I then calmed myself down and proceeded to explain the situation. "It's not quite what it looks like," I said. "This job was a favor to my fiancée's parents. I used all my own materials and vehicle. I can show you receipts in my company name to prove nothing was used from your stock."

He leaned back in his chair with a smug look on his face that says, "I caught you red-handed."

"Doesn't matter," he said. "You're doing a side job that should have been turned over to the company, a violation of company policy."

I was about to argue the point when I realized I would be wasting my time. This was the excuse he had been looking for to get rid of me. I didn't bother asking him details of how he knew or who took the pictures; it didn't matter now. He was nice enough to let us use the vans to get back home.

Rob and I killed the rest of the day discussing what we were going to do. We discussed it over a good bottle of rye.

I was shocked to hear the work van start up the next morning at seven sharp in my driveway. It was the boss. His wife had dropped him off at my place, so he could drive the van back to the office before work started.

I had parked my personal truck in front of the van, not knowing this would take place. I proceeded to throw some pants on to go outside and move my truck.

To my surprise, the big boss man decided the best way out of my driveway was to cut it sharp and go over the planter box. He then proceeded over my finely manicured lawn and snapped a few branches on the front tree! What an asshole!

Rob and I had talked about going to the Labor Relations Board for wrongful dismissal, but come Monday morning of the next week, Rob gets a phone call asking if he wants his job back. He, of course, said yes, so I guess he wasn't about to file a wrongful dismissal suit. Wow, talk about a one-sided event to get me fired!

The question remains: how did the boss and his wife even know we were doing that job? To my knowledge, the only person who knew about it was Roger. This is one of those situations where if it walks like a duck and talks like a duck . . . well, you know the rest.

I confronted him on it, and he looked me in the eye and swore he said nothing. I had hoped he would just come clean and admit he ratted me out, but he swore he did not. Roger had proven to me he was not a bullshitter or a liar in the time I had spent with him; why would he start now? Once again, it didn't matter anymore, so why waste time with it?

My fiancée quit, as it was obvious we were no longer wanted there. Roger and I kind of patched things up when the whole thing died down. We had a few more fishing outings together, but I haven't spoken to him in years now. Too bad, really. I learned the majority of my skills from him, and there are still days I wish he and I could be out on the lake fishing again. Perhaps at the conclusion of this book, I'll give him a call.

Rob and I remained close for some time. He often gave me a hand doing odd jobs and was a huge factor in helping me finish off the basement suite of my eventual new home. He began to get more involved with the girl he was dating, and soon, they were married. As usual, people get into the busy ups and downs of life and we just lost touch. Last I heard they have something like nine kids between them. Three from his first marriage, three from hers, and three of their own. I think they're trying to start their own baseball team!

I should look him up as well, one of these days, but there always seems to be something that takes priority. Wherever he is, I hope he's doing well; he deserves it.

It's interesting how, the older I get, the more I find that it's a small world.

A few months ago, a friend of mine who works in the heating industry was laid off. I recently phoned him to ask how his job hunting was going. He laughed and told me he went for an interview with a company called Energy-Save. I just about choked on my beer. My buddy, Brian, put me down on his resume as a reference. Apparently, my old boss chuckled when he saw my name and asked how I was doing.

"Is he still married?" was his question as he laughed.

I must admit it felt good for him to see my name as the boss of MY own company. I landed on my feet after he tried to cut me down, and I'm doing just fine.

Getting back to our story . . . this now leaves me and my fiancée without jobs. We are to be married in a few months, and this was not conducive to a good start.

She and her family were old school, and quite religious. They wanted us to get married in their church. In order to do so, we had to take marriage classes. Marriage classes? I had never heard of this before, but whatever, I guess. It was a couple of nights a week for a few weeks, and basically, I just showed up and listened.

My girlfriend smoked, so between sermons, lessons, and psalms, I would join the smokers outside and chat with whoever would listen to me. It was at one of these boring smoke sessions when we met a couple taking the same class.

I can't help but feel there is some kind of power that presents opportunities when they are needed, and that perhaps things happen for a reason.

I was chatting with this fellow who was puffing away, and he asked me what I do for a living. I tell him I'm in the plumbing, heating, and gas trade and his eyes light up. I figured he needed some work done at his home, but it was much better than that. He was an estimator for one of the bigger plumbing companies in the lower mainland of Vancouver. We'll change the name slightly, for legal reasons, and call them Mirani. I had heard of them but did not know much about them.

When he asked me about my experience, he pulled out a business card and said to come in for an interview the next day. He would talk to the owner and put in a good word for me. I showed up late morning as asked, and sat down for an interview. They looked at my resume and started asking me a few technical troubleshooting questions.

I'll always remember the big question. I was asked to go through the entire electrical sequence of how power gets transferred from the thermostat to the eventual zone valves and pumps on a hydronic system.

It was almost like a time warp, as I remembered Roger and me sitting at his kitchen table drinking beer as he drew a diagram and explained the whole process. I went into the sequence, using every professional and mechanical reference I could. After getting about three-quarters through the speech, I was told, "That's enough. I think you know more than I do about it." A great compliment to receive, especially on a job interview.

I received a call the next day to come in and get fitted for uniforms. I got the job! My fiancée eventually started working at her mom's shop and things were looking rosy again. Well, for a while at least.

Chapter 17

Don't Try This at Home, Kids

Mirani had one of the biggest crews I had ever worked for. They had a division strictly for drain cleaning, another for doing water mains, another for commercial work and building maintenance, and another for service work. (I've probably missed a few, but you get the point.) I was put into the service division and soon got to know the guys.

In service, one will also do installations of piping or, for example, hot water tanks. One of the guys I was paired with often was Dean.

Dean was a good looking, well-built guy who was soft spoken, but a really cool cat. He was always even-keeled; nothing really seemed to faze him. He almost reminded me of Rob.

One morning, he and I got the assignment to do a commercial-sized hot water tank. To put that in perspective, most people have a hot water tank in their home. Most are gas and are approximately forty U.S. gallons in capacity. They have a burner of about 30,000 BTU's—a unit of heat input measurement. Commercial tanks do the same job, but are much larger in size. They often are used to heat enough water for a large business or a small apartment complex. We're talking about ninety U.S. gallons with a burner of about 140,000 BTU's. They are about six feet in height and about three feet in diameter. When new, they weigh approximately four hundred pounds, but when the old ones get full of rust, sludge, and residual water, they often weigh well over five hundred pounds.

We go through the motions of draining the tank and getting the piping cut. The office has sent out a young kid with a pickup truck carrying the new tank. Our immediate job is to get the old tank out of this pit and out to the parking lot, before we can plan how to install the new one. This is quite a task for two guys and a young kid.

We have what's known as a fridge dolly. You have probably seen the average dolly Joe Homeowner uses to move a piece of furniture. Well, these are about seven feet tall, with multiple straps around them to hold down heavier loads.

We now have the tank strapped to the dolly and are about to move up the stairs into the parking lot. It doesn't seem like a big deal, and we honestly thought it wouldn't be. Boy, were we wrong.

Since Dean had a background in playing rugby, he had legs on him like tree trunks. We all agreed it would make sense for him to take the weight of the tank and handle the dolly. This young kid and I would be Dean's eyes, since his vision was blocked by the height and size of the tank. We would also help in the lifting of the tank up and over the steps.

Anyone who has ever used a dolly for heavy loads knows the secret is to allow all the weight of your object to rest at the centre point of the wheels on the dolly. You can attain this by finding the "sweet spot" where, at a certain angle, you can maneuver the object easily, as it is perfectly balanced with the weight over the wheels. When you stray from this point, you immediately feel how heavy your object is.

We were doing fine until we hit the top area, the last three steps. I lifted when I should not have, and Dean lost his balance. He fell back, and his legs and lower body were now pinned by the tank.

I heard him yell in pain as the tank pinned him in. I could feel the immediate rush of adrenaline through my veins, along with the sense of panic.

I said, "Are you okay?"

He quickly yelled back, "Get this fucking thing off of me!" You could hear the panic in his voice as he was struggling to free himself.

The problem now remained: how do I accomplish this task? I could not get to his side to help him, because there was no way around the tank. There was no other exit or entrance to this mechanical pit area. The only way to help him was to step over the tank to get to his side, and lift it enough so he could crawl free.

I told him, "Sorry, bud, but I have to do this."

I leapt on to the tank and heard him yell in sheer pain. The total weight on his leg at this point would be close to seven hundred pounds. To make matters worse, the young helper I had on my side of the stairs decides to follow suit. He proceeds to jump on the tank with me.

Poor Dean, one of those days he should have stayed in bed. I mustered enough energy to grab the handles and lift the tank, so Dean could crawl his way backward and free his pinned leg.

"Are you bleeding?" I asked.

"I don't think so, man. Just give me a few minutes to collect myself."

I immediately went to our dispatch radio and called the office. Our girl at the front desk answered, and I told her to phone for an ambulance, explaining what happened (not everyone had cell phones at this time).

She asked details of where we were located on the site and so on. When I came back to tell Dean help was on the way, he was hobbling about, trying to "shake it off" like an athlete would do after being injured. I was surprised he was even walking. I told him an ambulance was on its way, and he told me to cancel it. I told him he really should get that leg looked at for internal bleeding. He hobbled to the work van and told dispatch to cancel the ambulance.

He sat back and took a break to have a smoke. To my surprise, he then said, "C'mon, let's get this fuck'n tank in the truck."

He hobbled his way over to the tank that now lay on the stairs, and the three of us gave a few big grunts. We actually managed to get this old beast into the parking garage and the new one back into the pit for install. I finished the job at this point, and insisted he just rest in the truck. He was not going to take my advice and go to the hospital.

I drove him back to the office, where he was able to get into his own vehicle and go home. He didn't show up for the rest of the week. He returned the following Monday in shorts, with white bandaging wrapped around his upper thigh. His leg had about five days to heal, but when he removed the bandages to show me, I felt ill. His entire upper leg, from knee to groin, was various shades of purple, black, and blue. Wow!

He obviously suffered severe bruising and was lucky those big thighs took the weight without breaking. I'll tell ya, if it was me, it would have been a broken leg with crutches for months.

I asked him if he was pissed with me at all, and he laughed it off. He lived in the area where I lived, so I told him I would take him out for a few beers after work. I met him at a local pub that night. We watched a Canuck game and had wings and a few brews. We struck a friendship up that would end up being more valuable to me than I knew at the time . . . but we'll get to that.

Chapter 18

"You Won't Believe This Customer I Had Today"

As I stated earlier, one of the things I have always found interesting in this line of work is the people I've met over the years. Some good, some bad, and some that are just downright interesting.

I was still working for Mirani when I received the call to fix a few leaky pipes in a crawl space. Upon finishing the job, I produced a bill to the couple occupying the home to collect payment. The couple explained they were just the tenants, and that their landlord was responsible for payment.

So, I give the landlord a call to explain the situation. He asks all kinds of questions, and then explains I would have to come to his home for payment.

I asked him to just give me a Visa number, but he did not have a credit card of any kind. He explained if I wanted to get paid, I would have to come to his residence, where he would write me a check.

He was only able to go short distances, as he lived on his own and did not drive. I got his address and realized he did not live far from the current job site.

I radioed in to tell the office what I intended to do, and they were fine with it. It was the last call of the day anyway.

I arrived at this apartment building, and he buzzed me up to his suite. The place was in need of a good cleanup, but other than that, not bad for an elderly man getting around with a cane. I would peg him to be in his mid-to-late eighties.

He started asking me about the job and what I did. I explained, but he did not seem generally interested. His interests were to see what MY interests were. I realized this guy probably didn't get a lot of company, so I decided to just relax and chat with this old chap. Besides, I was in no hurry to go anywhere, and I probably wasn't going to get paid until I did.

He asked if I liked boxing. I said, "Ya, a little." I used to enjoy watching old reruns of Ali when he was in his prime.

"I used to be a promoter for all the big matches," he said. "I know Ali and his trainer, Angelo Dundee."

I began to question the validity of his stories at this point.

He mentioned he was also into horse racing, back in the day. He was involved with the Hastings Racecourse on the Pacific National Exhibition grounds, close to where I grew up. He had also been a promoter. I told him I had been there a few times, but horseracing wasn't my thing.

Then he asks me, "Who cuts your hair?"

I looked at him and said, "Uh, pardon me?"

He asked again. "Who cuts your hair?"

The honest answer was an old friend of my mom's who had a salon school on Hastings Street in Burnaby. "Marco Spags," I told him. "Why do you ask?"

He lets out this big belly laugh and tells me he taught Marco how to cut hair when he was a young kid. He proceeds to tell me he used to run a men's hair salon, and Marco started out by sweeping up the hair in the shop.

So, at this point, I'm thinking this poor old guy has missed his daily medication and is perhaps a few fries short of a happy meal. He sounded as if he had led quite the interesting life, but now he claims he knows my barber? I came to the conclusion perhaps this gentleman was just making up stories to keep me entertained, perhaps so I would stay longer. I don't know if he received a lot of visitors. How could he have taught the guy who cuts my hair? I'm sure I could have thrown any name out there and that would be the guy he taught.

It got worse.

It was a Saturday, as I was on a work shift that gave me Sundays and Mondays off. He asked me what my plans were after I left his place. I decided to appease him and just tell him exactly what I was doing. "Uh, well . . . I'm heading out to Richmond to see a friend of mine at a gathering called Wine Break."

He seemed interested and began to write the check. I figured if I kept explaining, he might actually stop asking questions and finally give me payment.

Allow me to explain Wine Break.

Earlier, I told you of my buddy, Kenny, whom I met when going to B.C.I.T. for plumbing school. He and his dad lived in a house in Richmond they rented from the owner, who lived next door.

The owner is one of the greatest guys you could ever want to meet. He is half Italian in heritage and makes the best homemade wine I have ever tasted. His name is Bobby and, if I had to guess, he's probably in his early seventies. Every Saturday—religiously—he holds a get together called Wine Break.

A chosen few, which make up the inner circle, are regulars. They show up at pretty much the same time every week, and it always turns into a great big bullshit session. He brings out the homemade wine, and the agreement is, everyone else brings appetizers, chips, or whatever.

Most of the guys are close friends of Bobby's and went to school with him when they were kids. But many are people he has met through this ritual gathering over the years. The age group would range from the forties through seventies. You can bring a friend to introduce to the group, but quite often, that friend will inevitably overindulge on the red wine and make an ass of themselves. Believe me, I have seen many a guy's girlfriend become pretty looped on the vino! They never get invited back.

Most of the regulars get called by their last names; there are even a few nicknames. I'm sometimes referred to as "Penguin," and we also have Larry the "Caveman." This guy is in his early seventies and still races cars down at Skagit Speedway in Washington. Amazing! He and I don't always see eye to eye, but I have the utmost respect for him.

I recall Caveman telling a story about the time he and his buddies decided to play a prank on their roommate. This would have been back in the late sixties. It sounds like he was quite the hell raiser when he was in his prime. They were out late one night at a dance, and upon leaving decided they were going to take a drive through Stanley Park to see what the night might have to offer.

Apparently, years ago there used to be a small zoo within the park. Well, that night, one of the baby kangaroos had escaped. He and his buddy, Roehouseur, chase down this kangaroo and somehow get it into their car. The intent was to drive the animal to their apartment, get it up the elevator, and into their sleeping roommate's bedroom.

The kangaroo was kicking and punching the backseats repeatedly. They made it to the apartment and attempted to get this erratic kangaroo into the elevator—easier said than done. This crazy animal would not go in, despite repeated attempts by Larry and his bud. They somehow managed to get it back into the car and drove to a nearby twenty-four hour Laundromat. By this time, it's about four a.m. An old woman arriving first thing in the morning to do laundry notices this bouncing kangaroo and decides to phone the police. They didn't believe her at first, but eventually came to rescue the "roo."

It made the papers the next day. The headlines said the kangaroo was kidnapped, but Caveman swears to this day that it was Hitchhiking! It is a great place to hear about cars, women, the political situations of the week, and some great old stories from a kinder and gentler era. It really is a one of a kind place to go. Cheers to you, Bobby!

Getting back to the old gentleman telling me stories, I was still waiting for the check.

"I know Wine Break!" He cleared his throat and said with confidence, "Bobby's my nephew. I know all about Wine Break."

Now he had my attention. I did not remember telling him Bobby's name. I passed it off, thinking I must have slipped it in to conversation without realizing it.

He then had the balls to tell me, "You tell him Uncle Al says hi."

I couldn't help but smile at this old guy and his "fictitious" world. I just felt comfort in knowing his world was a whole lot more exciting than mine. I grabbed the check and told him I would tell Bob he said hello.

I called into dispatch to finish my day and headed out to Wine Break. I sat down to enjoy the conversation and reflect on my busy week. After a few glasses, I started to smile thinking about this "crazy" old man.

Bob looks at me and says, "What the hell are you smiling about?"

I laughed and said, "You wouldn't believe me if I told you."

He smiled and said, "I'm old; not much surprises me anymore."

By this time, I had most everybody's attention, so I proceeded to say, "I just came from this customer's house to pickup payment for a job I did. This crazy old man goes on to tell me he knows Mohammed Ali, tells me he taught my barber how to cut hair, then proceeds to tell me he knows YOU!"

So of course, Bob asks me his name. I looked at him and said, "Uh, I think it was Al something."

Bob looked at me with that inquisitive brow, and said. "Al Principe?"

I said, "Ya, that was his name. How'd you know that?"

Bob looks at me with utmost seriousness, and says, "That's my uncle!"

Now, you have to understand, these guys are always playing tricks on each other, I assumed this was now one of those times. "Ya, whatever," I said. "Who put you up to this one, Kenny?"

"No, I'm not shitting you," He said. "He's really my uncle!"

To my complete and utter surprise, he proceeds to take out old photos of him and his Uncle Al working at the P. N. E., the Hastings Horse Races, and boxing photos with Jerry Quarry and Ali's trainer, Angelo Dundee. He proceeds to tell me Al was one of the most prolific and well-known entrepreneurs of his day. Everyone knew him. He had his own hair salon, his own booth at the Pacific National Exhibition, and dozens of other business ventures.

As my jaw lay open, looking at all these pictures of this great man I thought was just making up stories. Bob asks me, "So how the hell did you get to meet my uncle?"

I told him it was a long story, to which he replied, "Go ahead. I know where there's more wine."

Over the years, many people have come and gone from Wine Break. I myself have been going for more than fifteen years. Some celebrity types stop by now and then, as well. We often see Canadian Heavyweight Boxing champion Gord Racette. He was ranked thirteenth in the world at one point. He also held the world kickboxing title in the eighties and the world ju-jitsu title a few years back. For someone this adept at kicking the crap out of you, he sure is a great guy to joke around with. I recall having a few drinks with him one night and decided to test out a few wrestling moves. I remember hearing my neck crack when he had me in a "full nelson." What the hell was I thinking? He's a hulk of a man! I had a stiff neck for a week. He lives in the area and often stops by. In fact, he just phoned me a few weeks back, while having a glass of wine there, to wish me a happy birthday. I'm not sure what years he held the title but when you meet him in person, he's one hell of a big man. His forearms are about the size of my calves, and when he shakes your hand, you have a sense of what it must have been like to get a right hook from those meat paws.

Another great guy is Al Matsumoto. The name might not ring a bell, but whenever you see those championship sand carvings or snow carvings rest assured most of the really good ones are done by Al and his team. Some of his stuff is absolutely amazing. He is a very humble guy, but what a talent to see his craft. He gets paid to travel the world building these pieces of art. A sponsor will pay for his flight and accommodations to get him there, then he often comes in the top three in the judging. This means he leaves with prize money in his pocket. Must be nice getting paid to play in the sandbox!

As good as things were going at Mirani, they were not so good at home. I was now married, with a brand new house. We had moved out of the Surrey area of town and were now living in Maple Ridge. It's about an hour out of the big city of Vancouver. It was by far the biggest house I had ever lived in, and came with a big mortgage to boot.

We were only into the marriage a few months when my wife's biological father suddenly and unexpectedly passed away. It hit her family very hard, and I watched my wife go into a major depression. I tried to help, but there's not much anyone can do or say in a situation like this. I felt helpless. I was now the only one working, and the bills began to pile up. Looking back, I think we tried to buy our way to happiness, but we were only getting deeper into debt.

I guess when people aren't happy, they tend to try and fix the problem by purchasing lavish toys or taking big vacations to cover up the pain. This only masks the problem for a while, then the bills come in and it's twice as hard to pay them off. You are unmotivated and unhappy.

We were getting deeper into debt by the day. I had to start bringing in more money. The only answer I could think of was to see if I could get back into the union, where the money and benefits were much better. I made a few phone calls and was soon reinstated, paying my dues.

At this time, my buddy Dean was having some personal problems and was taking time off to get things in order. No one really knew what was going on with him, but most could tell he wasn't his regular self. I would often just say hello if I saw him in the mornings, but never really had a chance to find out what was wrong. Turns out, he was having troubles in his marriage as well. Our paths were closer to meeting than either of us knew.

Within a few weeks, I was called to start working at a union service company. I quit Mirani, and regrettably, left a lot of friends I had made.

Chapter 19

Back In the Union

In writing this chapter, I am struggling with whether or not to name the company I worked for. I have NOTHING good to say about them or the people I worked with, save for one. As much as I would like to dump every inch of shit I possibly can on them, I will choose the high road and leave them nameless. This book was not intended to be a "slam" session for my ego, but rather a good read that is uplifting and funny. I hope we all learn a thing or two about life in the end.

I recall the interview. It was downtown Vancouver in an expensive area of town. (Come to think of it, there aren't many inexpensive areas in Vancouver anymore.) You could just tell the clown interviewing me was a "suit" and probably had never lifted a tool in his entire life. But I bet he knew how to balance the books and make the shareholders happy. He liked the fact I was clean-cut and well-spoken. I was fitted for uniforms and asked to start on Monday.

I was a marked man with a target on my back, because the company I had just come from, Mirani, was one of their biggest non-union competitors. They were all anxious to see what I did and did not know. I was at a disadvantage, because this new company specialized in commercial and industrial building maintenance. I was much more adept at residential plumbing.

I'll never forget the first day. I was given a crew of apprentices, and my job was to install a commercial hot water tank in a mechanical room on the top of an apartment complex.

There is much planning that goes into this, as you have to secure the elevators and get the job done in the least amount of time possible. Your goal is to minimize the amount of inconvenience to the people who live there. It was on this morning I met my nemesis.

For this story, let's change his name to DICK, mainly because that's what he was.

This guy was like the ringleader of this band of assholes. He was the guy who obviously had his nose the furthest up the boss's ass. If you were buddies with him, you were in the inside looking out, not the other way around.

I'm trying to make a good impression on my first day and get this job done quickly and without mishap, especially remembering my last incident with the tank falling on my co-worker. Dick and his partner were there on the same day to do building maintenance and change the filters in the air handling units located on the roof. All the apprentices got out of their van and flocked to him to get the latest news and gossip on the company.

I'm not one of these "Let's sit around and have tea and crumpets" type of guys. There's a job to be done, so let's do it and we can have a couple of "pops" when the job is accomplished. I gave it a couple of minutes and then lost my cool. I sauntered over and gave them all a bit of a dirty look. Dick says to me, "Good morning! You must be the new guy."

He always seemed to have this shit-eating grin on his face that always made him look like a cheap used car salesman.

"Ya," I said. "And you must be Dick. Hey, hope you don't mind, but I need to break up your tea party to get some fuck'n work done."

Everybody looked at me and a couple of eyebrows were raised. It was the feeling of high school when a kid tells you to meet him in the courtyard for a fight after class. What was the big deal? Apparently, no one had the guts to tell this asshole what they thought.

"Of course," he said. "Wouldn't want to slow you down. I'm sure we'll see each other around."

This was probably not the wisest move to make on my part if I wanted a smooth ride in this company, but looking back now, it would not have mattered what I did; they were all out to make my life miserable.

The next morning, I arrived at work to get pulled aside by the dispatcher. He was another pain in the ass, but he was the owner's son, so not much could be said to him if you wanted to keep your job. It, once again, was a company with the motto of "It's not what you know, but who you know."

It used to piss me off how everyone walked on eggshells around him and kissed his ass. I was asked if I had experience with a plunger. I said yes. Apparently, this was the wrong answer, as I was then told the men's washroom in our lunchroom had a plugged toilet.

Since I was now low man on the totem pole, I was picked to unplug it. I was about to suggest one of the apprentices do it, but I kind of figured this was a bit of a test and I needed this job. So, I shut up and got to it.

It was obvious someone had done this purposely. They had taken a large bowel movement, and then proceeded to plug the toilet with paper towel. Once you flush, everything gets plugged. What a mess! This had my buddy Dick written all over it.

But it wasn't just one time, oh no. This went on all week. Finally, on Friday morning, the suit who hired me came into the men's washroom as I was plunging and auguring. He asked how I was making out in my first week.

"Just peachy," I replied, as I was wrist deep in shit.

"You're doing well. I realize certain guys are making it hard for you here. Don't let them get to you."

Easy for him to say, he hadn't cleaned toilets all week.

I was now miserable at work and miserable at home. Things were not getting better in my marriage, and it seemed no matter how hard I tried, I just could not catch a break with this new job.

You could just tell most guys did not want to work with me, and when someone did not want to go on call, I was the one chosen. The paychecks were nice, but was it all worth it?

A few weeks had gone by and I was driving to a job in the New West area of town. I was in a hurry, so was looking down at my map book. (We did not have GPS.) I was glancing toward the left side of the van when I noticed traffic starting to move. Without looking up, I released my foot from the break to start moving with traffic. My face was still in the map book when my van came to a very sudden halt, the type you get when you hit the bumper of the person in front of you!

Great! Apparently, the lane to my left was the left-hand turning lane. They had the green arrow; my lane did not.

The two of us drove to the nearest parking lot to exchange insurance info. Now I had to radio in to dispatch to tell them why I was late for the job. Everyone listening to their dispatch radio was about to hear I had a fender bender, but I honestly didn't care anymore.

Since the parking lot I was in was a McDonald's, I decided that, if I was going to be late for the call, I might as well grab some lunch. Here's where the story gets even better.

I proceed through the drive-thru, then parked and enjoyed my lunch in the van. After gathering myself and letting my food digest, I decided to get back on the road. I checked my rear and side mirrors to ensure there was no one behind me. I proceeded to pull out and, wouldn't ya know it . . . BAM! I did it again.

I had backed into some young kid in a delivery van attempting to exit the lot. He was obviously going too fast, but I would still be to blame. But once again, I no longer cared.

To my surprise, this kid was in a bit of a panic. If I remember correctly, he said something about it being his dad's van and he was already on probation. He asked if we could just let this one go, as there was minimal damage to each vehicle. Well, this suited me just fine. I made it sound like I was pissed off and

144

hesitant about it, but we both drove away not reporting it. Wow, did I finally catch a break?

As fate would have it, sadly, no. It was merely a couple of weeks later when I was driving down a busy main road, when the transmission on the van decided to crap out. There I was, stuck on the side of the road. I called in to dispatch and asked if they could call a tow truck, and a cab to get me home.

I just knew when the van got towed back to the shop someone was going to go through the van with a fine tooth comb to see if they could nail me with something. I don't do drugs, so there was no worry about finding pot or any other type of drug; I never drank on the job, so I was not worried about beer cans. But, they had always told us that we had to call in to dispatch if we were stopping for lunch. This even meant the drive-thru. So as I glanced around the van, there were tons of wrappers and bags from A&W, Wendy's, and McDonald's. I would not put it past them to reprimand me for this, so I decided to get rid of the evidence.

I put them all into one bag and waited for a break in the traffic. Now, listen, kids, I do not condone littering! It is a disgusting thing to do and pollutes the environment!

But just this once, I decided to throw the bags into the bushes. Just when I thought the coast was clear, I tossed them, only to have a truck come by via the off ramp, and see me toss garbage into the woods.

The guy rolled down his window, yelled some obscenity, and gave me the finger. What I did not realize was the company name and phone number was plastered on the van. Once again, just my luck, this guy decided to phone into the office to report me. One more nail in my coffin as far as employment with this firm went.

I could go on with more incidents, but I'm starting to get depressed just writing about it, and that was eleven years ago! Needless to say, I lasted there about eight months before I was let go. They at least waited until I had enough weeks to collect unemployment insurance. How nice.

I recall taking my personal belongings out from the service van. They actually had one of the managers there to watch me, ensuring I didn't take any of their precious belongings.

I swore upon leaving that shit hole if I ever seen my buddy "Dick" outside of business hours, or in a back alley, I would knock his teeth out.

There was one guy who was an apprentice when I worked there. He was one of the "in crowd," but I always felt he liked and respected me. On my last day, he shook my hand and said this to me, "You were one of the nicest guys I've ever met working here. Unfortunately, that isn't what you want to survive around this place. Good luck."

I'll always remember that. It made me feel good that I was still the person I was when I started; I hadn't let the wolves change me.

There was another guy, a foreman in the construction division, who I got to know briefly. He was a great guy and helped me in areas when I needed assistance. Years later, I would receive a call from this old age pensioner that had no heat. She was, and still is, one of my nicest customers. She tells me her son-in-law would usually do this, but he is so busy, and she did not want to bother him. I asked who he worked for. Guess who it was? My old foreman. She shows me a picture of him and her daughter on their wedding day. Small world—I told her to say hello from me.

Keeping on the same track, you sometimes get re-acquainted with those you didn't like. While writing this story, a few weeks back, my (now) wife tells me she is going for brunch with her girlfriends. Her old schoolmates usually get together every few months for drinks, lunch, and to talk about shoes, purses, and whatever else it is women talk about.

She comes home and I, of course, ask her how her lunch was. She proceeds to tell me it was great, and a girl she has known since kindergarten decided to join the brunch.

I was paying half-assed attention until she mentioned her friend was divorced now, but seeing this new guy who's also in the plumbing and heating field.

"Oh, ya?" I said. "What's his name?"

She thinks for a second and says, "Uh . . . DICK, I think it was. Yes, that's right."

I turned my head slowly and asked if she caught a last name of this guy.

"Well, no. Why do you ask?"

I smiled and said, "No reason. I just know a lot of people in the industry."

I mean, really . . . what are the chances, right?

Next day, my wife is at work and sends me an email. She is now keeping in touch with this old friend and had asked what her new guy's last name was. She sends me the reply email.

Sure as shit, it's my old nemesis, Dick! And, to boot, there's a picture of him and her hugging lovingly as they play on the beach. He still has that shit-eating, used car salesman smile! What a piece of work.

I wanted to print the picture so I could throw darts at it, but figured I was beyond that in maturity (barely). At the bottom of the email, it said "Maybe me, Dick, you, and your hubby can get together some time."

Fat chance that's happening. Not unless I can bring Guido and his fat cousin Vinnie with baseball bats to have a chat with him, if ya know what I mean. Buddagoish!

I explained the past work history to my wife, and she emailed her friend back telling who I was. She also said to tell DICK that I gave him a big hello.

The email replied with, "Ya, Dick remembers Kevin. Said they used to work together."

Kind of makes it sound like we were best buds at the shop, doesn't it? Almost brings a tear to my eye.

Funny, my wife hasn't heard back from her since.

Chapter 20

Ch-Ch-Ch-Ch-Changes
(Turn and Face the Strain)

I shopped my name around a few union shops and was soon picked up by Honeywell. These guys are huge and known the world over. I was treated well there, but must admit most of the work they did was beyond my capabilities. I learned a lot from the guys I was paired up with, about commercial boilers and air handling units. That knowledge comes in handy today, but at that time, Honeywell was not the fit or future career path for me.

So now I was out of work again and things were at the breaking point with my marriage. Anyone who has been through this knows that, at the end of a hard day, you just want to come home to your family and loved ones. When your home is a place you want to avoid at all costs, changes have to be made. Sometimes, deciding what to do and where to go are the hardest decisions to make.

I knew deep down I wanted to start my own business again. I had been reading books on tax strategies and how to run a successful small business. I now felt I had the professional knowledge and the desire, but how could I focus on a business and massive career shift when my personal life was an absolute mess? I knew things had to change, but where to start?

This is where I firmly believe there are powers in this world greater than we are, and that maybe, just maybe, things happen for a reason. I believe Karma and positive energy will come back to you, if you give it out on a consistent basis.

If you choose to get technical about it, there is proof of this as well. Einstein proved energy is neither created nor destroyed; it is simply passed on from one entity to another. Therefore, the positive energy you emit in action and thought is out there to, perhaps, and/or eventually, come back to you. Just as throwing a ball against a wall takes your energy to move the ball, that same energy brings it right back to you.

After a huge screaming session with my wife, I just had to leave the house to clear my mind and figure out what my next move was. I decided to drive to a local pub and grab a six-pack. My intent was to find a quiet spot, have a few, and calm down enough to think rationally. As I walk to the counter of the pub for off sales, I hear, "Hey, Kevin. How are you, man?"

I turned around to see my buddy Dean from the Mirani days having a beer with a friend.

"Holy shit, how are you, bud? Great to see you."

With that, I sat down and we caught up on life and the ups and downs we were both going through. It turns out he was going through a worse time than I was. He was having trouble with his wife, which was what I had assumed was happening when he was taking personal time off work. He came home one day to find his wife had packed up the furniture, dishes, and all else . . . and was gone. She had also taken the kids with her, and he had no idea where they were. She was not taking or returning any of his phone calls, and all the mutual friends they had were telling him nothing.

I can't imagine how that must have felt, not knowing where your kids are, or if they are safe. Just having your whole world taken away from you in an instant –wow!

At the time of our meeting, he had recently found their whereabouts and was dealing through lawyers to settle his divorce proceedings. He was still living in the house nearby my residence.

I felt almost sheepish telling him about my piddly problems, but he listened intently and genuinely cared about my circumstance. I told him I knew I had to get out of this marriage, but did not know what to do and where to start.

It was at this point the biggest door opened that would change my life.

Dean looked at me and said, "I know what you're going through." He then took his key ring out of his pocket and began to remove a few keys. He grabbed a coaster with a pencil and wrote down a set of numbers. "Here are the keys, address, and security code to the house. If things get too heavy, pack up your shit, and you can live at my place. I've got a spare bedroom and lots of room if you need to store anything. Make yourself at home."

I asked him if he was sure about this, and he stated he could use the company. I guess being alone in that house was driving him a little crazy. I thanked him, and eventually returned home that night with the attitude of giving it one more shot.

It was one week later, and I had definitely had enough. I seem to recall her going out for lunch with her mom or something, so I took the opportunity to gather my personal stuff and head over to Dean's place. I called him on his cell to make sure the offer still stood, and he seemed genuinely happy about my decision.

I arrived to find him standing at the door with a cold beer in his hand for me. I thought to myself, *Hmm . . . maybe this isn't going to be so bad after all.*

I finally got settled in, and after a week or so I started to feel like my old self again. Stress is a much bigger factor in one's health than I think most people realize. I can tell you one thing: I did not have one grey hair on my head until I went through this whole ordeal.

I sought legal advice and was soon on my way to the wonderful, happy place that is divorce. Such fun! I am being sarcastic, of course. It was without a doubt the worst ordeal of my life. But, Dean and I made the best of our situations.

We both dabbled in playing guitar, and both loved the same type of music. He introduced me to some great bands, and I ended up buying an old, used guitar. He and I would jam some nights over a few beers. I wasn't working and neither was he at the time, so we had not much else to do.

I noticed he had a hot tub outside, and it looked like it was not in use. It was now the middle of summer and, since we had a place to ourselves, I thought it only natural to have a hot tub in full operation at party central. He explained to me the gas to his home had been shut off by the local utility company. The account was in his ex-wife's name, and he was not able to pay the fees she had racked up to get the system re-connected. He had been able to move the lock just enough to get gas flow through the shut-off valve and allow us hot water for showers and such. He didn't have a lot of gas knowledge, so wasn't sure about firing up the hot tub.

I looked over the heat exchanger and soon had the unit fired up. Next night we were enjoying the hot tub and having a few drinks. Yee haw!

Unfortunately, there will always be someone out there who is hell bent on ruining someone else's good time. Within twenty-four hours of us partying that night, the local gas company came on to his premises and removed the meter entirely.

Turns out, the neighbors were good friends with his ex and called to tell her of our good time. She obviously called the gas company, asking how we were able to do this without a gas connection. How nice of her.

Now that the meter was gone, all that remained was a gas pipe sticking out of the ground. Dean was the first to notice this when he arrived home and gave me a call.

"What do we do now?" he said.

I chuckled and told him, "Don't worry about it. I'll have the gas back on by tonight. And invite some ladies over for the weekend; that hot tub's gonna be heated, bud!"

Okay, kids, what I am about to tell you, I in no way condone or endorse. I realize it was not a smart thing to do and, as a licensed gas fitter, I should not be doing such reckless and immature actions; but just this once!

Because I had commercial gas knowledge, I knew the underground gas pressures. I also had some leftover parts from that job at the hotel, and proceeded to dig through a box of old parts in my pickup truck.

I proceeded to go back to the house, hooked up the appropriate regulator, and piped the gas back to the house. Within no time, I had the system up and running. Having the hot tub running was just a bonus, but we needed hot water for showers and to do dishes. No ex-wife was going to ruin our fun, so I thought.

We had a great time that weekend, and Dean was still in shock I was able to make it work. What happened on Monday was something I did not expect, nor even think possible.

I will assume the nosey neighbor caught wind of our antics and, once again, phoned the local utility company. I would have loved to see the gas utility representative when he looked over the fence to see my handiwork. Apparently, he was not as impressed with it as I was, and immediately had a crew come in with a backhoe and shovels.

I was not home at the time, but they succeeded in digging down to the gas line, and installed a separate shut-off on the city side of his property. There was nothing left but a cap on the lawn just outside his fence, with a lock on it we were NOT going to break. The fun was over. The gas company was obviously not impressed and flexed their muscle. Welcome to cold showers. Guess I kinda had it coming.

I took this as a sign that summer, and party time, was coming to an end. Fall was around the corner, and people start to have their furnaces tuned up. The cold weather always brings around problems to heating for those who have been negligent in servicing.

I started the wheels in motion for getting back to work, but did not want to go back to the union. So, where to now?

My living situation was about to change, as Dean's divorce was forcing him to sell the house. The bonus was that the real estate woman he hired was an absolute knock-out. Wow! Just gorgeous! I asked him where he knew her from, and he admitted he just picked the best-looking one out of the real estate weekly newspaper. He's such a dog!

I casually looked in the local papers for basement suites, but nothing looked as if it was a good fit. But once again, things happened for a reason.

I received a phone call that weekend from my old neighbor. He tells me his cousin's water line has burst from the city main. He doesn't know any plumbers, and anyone he calls is going to charge big bucks for a weekend service call. Would I be interested?

Well, I always try to be there when people really need me. I feel that one day, I might need a hand and I hope someone is there for me.

I arrived to find an absolute mess. The entire basement was flooded. I introduced myself and got straight to work on getting the water up and running. The cousin seemed like a good guy, kind of a hunting, fishing sort of guy. I soldered up a new water line connection, and he was good to go in no time. He took a break from sopping up the flood water and offered me a cold beer. I knew I would like this guy!

As we get to talking, he states he is not only pissed off about the mess, but that he was going to put an ad in the paper that weekend to rent out the basement suite. As I heard this, my ears raised up like my dog when you say the phrase, "Go for a walk?"

I looked around the place and started to inquire about the suite. I asked him what he wanted per month, and he smiled and said," Why, do you know somebody who might want to move in?"

I explained my situation of needing a place, and when he asked how much my plumbing bill was, I told him to take it off my first month's rent. We both had a good laugh and shook hands. I moved in a couple of weekends later.

The rather creepy thing about this was it was only one block from my marital home that my ex-wife was still living in. We were now separated, but I still had to pay all the bills, as she was not working. I tell ya, divorce is one of the most fucked up things to go through. Nobody really wins, and it's a steel-toed kick to the crotch to see the house you worked so hard to maintain just wasting away waiting for all the issues to be settled. You can only hope that the next people to buy it have better luck than you did.

After settling into my new digs, I decided to give my old buddy Mags a call. It was mainly just to catch up and shoot the bullshit, but I also dropped the hint that I was looking for work. What happened next was yet another example of things happening for a reason. I'm not sure if it's just good timing, or if it's just good karma, but doors began to open for me, and I ran with the opportunities to see where they would take me.

Chapter 21

Mags and the Penguin: The New Dynamic Duo!

Mags had been doing well, running his own company for quite some time at this point. He had worked his way into favor with many of the local wholesalers. They were giving his business cards out when people needed a good reliable plumber.

He was at a point where he was only advertising in the local church tabloid and word of mouth. Mags is Italian, so he had much of the local Italian community calling him for business.

We chatted for a while and I told him what had been going on in my life, and that I was wondering where I should pursue work. He told me he was now so busy he could not keep up with his service calls. Mags knew of my background in this area and started thinking of a master plan. The main bond the two of us had was utmost trust in each other. The biggest risk you're taking when someone works for or you is the chance he secretly tells your customer he has his own business and can do the work cheaper. He hands your customer his card, and next thing you know, you have lost your clientele and can't figure out why.

I explained all I had was a pickup truck at the time, and not even a full-size one. That didn't matter to Mags; he was never about the show, always about the quality and doing the job right. We soon had a basic agreement in place for working together.

I would have my truck stocked with basic plumbing and heating parts. Any stock used on his customers from my truck I would purchase on his account to pay me back. He would phone me the night before to give me a list of the customers' names and addresses. He would also tell me the nature of the jobs and what I may, or may not, need to pick up. It was brilliant!

Mags was very attentive to detail and made my life easy. Because we were such good friends, it was easy to work together.

The difficult part comes when you begin to mix money with friendship. I can honestly say the saying is true—the two rarely mix—and it is one of the hardest things to do. Although they were his customers, it was still my labor, my gas, my wear and tear on the vehicle, and my tools. So, what is a fair price for him to pay me? I was not driving a proper van that could carry a full set of parts, so I was at a disadvantage, and that meant not being able to ask for a regular rate.

We finally agreed on a price that was a little on the low side for my liking, but it was at least an opportunity to get back into the groove and work for a guy I highly respected.

Things started out well. I met many customers that had dealt with Mags for many years, and they were all nice people. I could not help but notice a good majority of them were Italian; many of them from the neighborhood we grew up in.

I remember going to one house about three blocks from our old high school and stomping grounds. She was an old, Italian widow with many graduation pictures of her kids on the surrounding walls. We struck up a conversation and I told her I used to live a few blocks up the road. Her eyes lit up and she asked what school I graduated from. It was the same as her kids. She told me all their names, and then went into asking if I knew them. Most, I did. My very first girlfriend lived on the same block, and I asked if she knew the family. She did, and next thing you know I was pretty much part of the family.

She started rambling off every Italian niece and nephew she had and what school they went to. I then stated all the Italian friends I grew up with, and she knew most of them. Then as she was pretty much ready to make me a big Italian supper with all the family invited, she looked me in the eye and asked, "So, are you Italian?"

I looked at her smiling face and hesitantly replied, "Uh . . . well . . . no."

The smile disappeared from her face and she said to me, "Oh, well, that's 'a too bad."

Don't get me wrong; I'm sure she meant nothing against me, but was clearly sad I was not from the old country back home.

I guess I was no longer part of the family but it was okay; for a moment or two, I felt what it was like to be in a nice, Italian family. Mags and I still get a good laugh when I tell that story around friends.

Some customers were not so inviting though. Mags often worked in some of the ritzier neighborhoods in the lower mainland. He is very adept at high end renovations and often gets work in very expensive homes.

I had to do a gas line for a woman who lived in such a place, and she definitely gave the impression to me her shit didn't stink, pardon the expression. I look back now and understand I probably did not look all that professional, driving up in a weighed-down pickup truck without company lettering. But one should not judge a book by its cover.

She proceeded to ask me if I was ticketed for such work, and how long I had been in the business. In fact, at one point, I remember her asking me if I knew what I was doing. I felt a very strong urge to politely put my work boot in her ass, but decided to show her who the intelligent one was. It was time to play a little game.

I proceeded to politely get her attention as she was yapping on the phone to her broker or whomever. She acknowledged my presence, and I told her in my ever so sweet and polite tone, "Uh, we have the gas line cut open; just wanted to ensure that you did phone the utility company and have them shut your main gas line off."

She looked at me with slight disdain and said, "Phone the what? No, I did not."

I then came in with the slight panic-stricken voice and said, "Okay, are you serious, ma'am? You have not phoned to make arrangements for the gas to be shutdown?"

The look on her face was priceless; it was that look a deer gets when it's staring into the lights of the oncoming truck. "Oh my God, no one told me I had to do that!"

She abruptly told whoever was on the phone she had to go, and jumped off her chair. Now I had her attention.

"What do I do? Who do I phone?" she shouted.

I had a look of panic and I stated, "Let's not panic. It's too late to phone the utility company. I need you to get on the phone and immediately phone 911. Give them your address and just tell them Code Red. Tell them Code Red!"

In a complete panic, she grabbed the phone and I actually heard her say, "Nine-one-one. Nine-one-one. What's their number?"

I could not continue to torture this lady any longer, and I was now smiling and attempting not to laugh. I walked up to her as she was frantically looking in the phone book and told her to calm down. I laughed and told her it was fine. I had the main shut off and there was nothing to worry about—no need to call 911. Her face was rather pale and flushed as she asked if we were going to blow up. I told her I had everything under control and that the job was actually completed.

I explained she wasn't very respectful in some of her comments towards my professionalism, and that I was just trying to lighten the situation a little. She was not amused (weird!) and did not talk to me much after that. (Bitch!)

That night, I received the routine phone call from Mags for the next day's work. I was asked what happened on the job site. Apparently, little miss snobby phoned the office to complain about me. (Can't figure out why.) I received a bit of a verbal wrist slapping from Mags, but she had it coming. We both laugh at that one now.

Some of the best times were when the two of us worked together. We used to be on the same job site back in the union days, but never had the chance to work side by side. Now, it was different, as we often worked together, laughing about the good times growing up. I learned a lot working with Mags.

We had one job out in the Burnaby area where we had grown up. It was a huge house, and Mags and I were doing all the in-floor radiant heating tubes for hot water hydronic-style heating. We were on ladders most of the day and pulling pipe through pre-drilled holes. At one point, our favorite song came on the shitty old radio we had playing. Mags cranks up the volume, and the next thing you know, he and I are dancing and singing at the top of our lungs on the ladders.

Now, you have to picture this. Here are two professional journeyman tradesmen, charging big money for doing a very tedious job. We are supposed to be poised and professional, but we are acting like school girls at a slumber party. At that point, the homeowner comes around the corner to check on the progress of the home. I can only imagine what went through his head as he sees two grown men singing and dancing on ladders. It's Murphy's Law that states anything that can go wrong will go wrong. The whole week, we hadn't seen this guy, and of all times, he picks that very moment to show up. Mags turns down the radio and I slowly come down from the top rung of the ladder to explain sheepishly, "Uh . . . I'm gonna just go to the truck and . . . uh . . . get that thing you needed." The homeowner was not amused.

Speaking of the top rung, Mags and I used to be big wrestling fans when we were kids. I remember being devastated as a kid when I found out it was fake. I felt ripped off! I felt like my time was wasted cheering for Hulk Hogan and feeling bad when he would get slammed to the canvas by Andre the Giant. And all along, they were faking it. Bastards!

Anyway, we would often watch the low budget wrestling from the Calgary area of Canada called Stampede Wrestling.

A lot of big names went on from there to the WWE, like Brett Hart, Davy Boy Smith, and The Dynamite Kid. There was even lower budget wresting that I remember, filmed locally in Vancouver at the old BCTV studios in Lake City. I believe it was called All-Star Wrestling, a collection of the biggest freaks and lowlifes in the industry. I guess you had to start there and work your way up. There were some big names that made the local circuit, like Don Leo Jonathan and Gene Kinisky. If I remember, Jake the Snake Roberts wrestled there to start his career and eventually made it to the big time.

There was this character we used to imitate from the Stampede days. He was this crazy Japanese guy named K.Y. Wakamatsu. I think he was somebody's manager and always had this big bamboo stick that he would use to stop an opponent from pinning his guy. He would just come out of nowhere and crack a guy over the back with this big bamboo pipe. The announcer, Ed Whalen, would yell, "OH, Wakamatsu off the top rope!"

If anyone has ever seen the Pink Panther movies with Peter Sellers, they will remember his sidekick, Cato. The character Cato was actually hired by the detective, Clouseau, to hide in various closets, or behind the drapes, and attack the inspector. He felt this kept his wits sharp. Well, I was like Cato, and Mags was my Inspector Clouseau.

I would play K.Y. Wakamatsu by finding a cardboard tube or old broom handle, anything I could find at the job site. I would wait for Mags to enter a room. Often, I would be hiding, and then boom! Wakamatsu jumping out of a closet, or from behind the customer's drapes, to come down over his back with the bamboo (cardboard) stick. It used to drive him nuts.

I recall the last time I did it. The cardboard tube I used was a little on the thick side, with some pretty good weight behind it. It was all I could find and I did not intend to really hit him that hard with it. I called Mags into the room to find out what size pipe he wanted me to use, and off the ladder I flew.

I yelled, "Wakamatsu, off the top rope!"

I kinda lost my balance, and Mags zigged when I thought he would zag. Next thing you know, WHAM! I was aiming for his back, but caught him across the back of the neck. Ouch! Good thing Mags is built like a brick shit house, and that he is a great friend, because that one must have hurt.

I looked at him with my eyes wide open, not knowing if he was going to power slam me or bear hug me until I stop breathing. He turned around and looked at me with this crazy look that kinda said, "Okay, Penguin. It's my turn."

He kneeled down to pick up the broken tube. I shit you not, I ran so fast out of that room I think a smoke trail was left on the carpet in my path.

That was the last time I ever did that.

Soon, our team was flourishing. With Mags's finishing knowledge, and my heating and gas knowledge, we were busy and both making money. I was now working for him on a steady basis and knew this was the avenue for me to follow as a career path.

I renamed my company. If I was going to be taken seriously, I had to loose the Penguin. Mags was now paying me as a subcontractor, which meant I would invoice him for the work I had done and he would pay me under a company account. This now opens up a whole different way of doing business that incurs legal changes.

I soon had my own insurance, business accounts at the bank, my own accountant, and was paying into legal entities, like the Workers Compensation Board. I purchased a business license and registered my name with the government. It was a lot of red tape, but I was now able to take advantage of all the tax write-offs a business enjoys. It's very complicated, but the books I had read years before about beating the taxman really helped. Finding a good accountant is also a huge asset.

One issue of concern was that Mags was not able to supply me with enough work to keep me busy eight hours a day, five days a week. He knew of a few other guys in the industry running their own small businesses, and he introduced me to them. The idea was for everyone to network. If Mags did not have any work for me on a particular couple of days, he would phone the other companies and see if they could keep me busy. This system worked well for a while.

At this time, I decided I needed to get out of the pickup truck and into a real van.

I had my eye on a van that was clearly used, but still looked in relatively good condition, at one of the local used vehicle shops. This place looked kind of seedy, but after talking to the manager, the place didn't seem all that bad. Boy was I wrong.

It had a new coat of shiny white paint; to cover the rust, I found out. It was already equipped with a foam insulation that had been sprayed inside the van. This was great, in that it kept the heat in and lessened the noise of the road. The odometer read just over 300,000 kilometers. This was a little high, but not too bad I thought. The funny thing is I did not notice on the test drive the gauge had stopped working. This meant the old clunker was at least driven up to 300,000, but how many more after the odometer stopped? It was in pretty rough shape in areas, but with the new tires and paint job . . . it was what I needed and all I could afford.

They gave me a trade-in straight across the board. My Ford Ranger for this old GMC work van. I somehow think they got the better of that deal, but one has to do what one has to do. I went to an auto wrecker and was able to get some shelving out of an old van that had met its fate with what looked like a telephone pole. They were cheap, and over a few beers that weekend, I had all the shelving in and parts stocked. I was now ready to look professional and get a little more respect for my business.

Now that I was able to carry more parts and not look so "cheesy," I decided to ask Mags for a raise in pay. I felt I deserved it and had worked hard to earn it. It was a rather odd situation I was in at this point. I had all the amenities to go completely on my own without Mags, but I did not have a steady clientele to keep the jobs coming in. Mags did, so I really had nowhere else to go if I did not like what he was paying me. It was either do as he said, or go back to working as an employee for someone again. I had come too far to go back to that.

At anytime during our negotiation process, Mags could have just said, "Well, Penguin, if you don't like what I'm offering, you can find somewhere else to work."

He had that option, but being the classy guy he is, he never left me out to dry; he always listened to my points of view, and did what he thought was fair. We eventually agreed on a bigger wage for my services, but there are so many factors that came into it. Should I be credited for my travel time to his job sites? Should I charge travel time to pick up parts for his jobs? Or does this get worked into my hourly rate? It was becoming ever more complicated and was starting to put pressure on our professional friendship.

The problems between us started to arise when I began to get phone calls for doing jobs on my own. Since I lived in a different municipality than Mags, I was starting to get noticed around town, and was getting work for myself. This was tempting, as now I was able to charge full rate for my own jobs, and my bank account was starting to grow. I also had the other companies that Mags had introduced me to calling me for more work. I was now doing work for Mags, myself, and two other companies. It was becoming too much, and something had to give.

There was one company owner Mags had introduced me to; his name was Stan. This guy was a real go-getter and knew how to talk the talk. Whether he could walk the walk was another story. Stan's company began to grow rapidly, and I like to think he noticed my talents.

I remember getting a phone call from him one day. He and I met for beers at the local pub. We sat down, and he told me how much his company was growing and his visions for the future. He stated he liked what he had seen in the way I handled myself, and my workmanship. Stan had more experience in the heating end of the trade, and his company was focused more to this end of the spectrum.

Out of the two portions of the trade, I must admit, I enjoy heating more. The work allows you to use your head a little more as opposed to manual labor, and there is good money to be made on selling parts. Stan was as good as a used car salesman, or a politician with the talk. This guy could sell an ice cube to an Eskimo. He was very good with the sales pitch, and I sometimes think he missed his calling in life. It was somewhere between our fifth or sixth pint of beer when he floored me by asking, "So, what's it gonna take to get you away from Mags, and start working for me full time?"

I was shocked and decided to sober up and be cautious with what I said. I opted to roll with it and ask him what type of money we were talking about. I don't remember all the aspects of that conversation, but I do remember telling him what I thought I should be making per hour. To my surprise, he answered, "Done! Call Mags and tell him I get first billing to book you for work."

Wow, how tempting was this! I must admit, it was great to have someone say I was worth what I was asking. There were no debates or squabbling, just a compliment and an agreement to pay me what I wanted. I would still be paid as a contractor with checks made out to my company name. This guy was really busy and could give me about thirty hours a week. The other ten hours, I could pick up with customers of my own. I could be making more money than I had ever made.

But, one has to remember loyalty and friendship. It was Mags who got me into this great situation; it is not right to just abandon ship at the first sign of someone dangling the money carrot in front of you.

I was a little on the desperate side of needing money, as my wife and I were now going through the divorce proceedings, and paying bills on two households was tapping me out. A lawyer I spoke to had told me even though I was not living in my marital home, I should continue to pay all the bills for a few months, to prove good faith if things go to court. How fucked up is that?

I told Stan I would definitely consider his offer and get back to him, but I would not be cutting Mags out of the picture in any way. He understood and respected that decision. He paid the bar tab, and we shook hands in the faith of doing more work together in the near future.

I was now on the brink of making the comeback I had always wanted since Penguin Plumbing went down. I just had to be careful, and not make any knee-jerk decisions, especially ones based on a greed for money. Thinking long term seemed to be the wise choice, but how was I to juggle work for two different contractors and not lose business for myself?

Chapter 22

Trying To Keep My Sanity

After much thinking about the situation, I decided to just let the chips fall as they may. It was first come, first serve. Whoever called me first to book me for a job, that's who I booked for my services.

I was still trying to do the occasional calls that came in for my own company, but I had to be careful and not tell the other contractors for fear of ruffling feathers, so to speak. It became exhausting trying to fit these jobs in on weekends and after hours. I had magnetic plaques made with my company name and logo on them. They were great; I was able to put them on the side of my van when I was doing my own jobs, then take them off when doing a job for Mags or Stan. But honestly, what a pain in the ass it was always having to remember who I was working for all the time.

With all the miles I was putting on, I was finding it hard to keep up the maintenance on this old van I had purchased. The alignment must have been out, as my tires were severely wearing on one side. It was starting to burn a bit of oil, and I constantly had to keep an eye on that. The rust covered by the paint job was also starting to show through. The shitty thing was I hadn't owned it very long.

The worst problem was that, every now and then, it would just die as I went to accelerate. Honestly, I would literally be at a stop light and attempt to proceed on the green, then the van would just die. It would always restart, but I could not help but think this could be dangerous.

How right I was to be.

It was a few weeks of crazy hours when I decided to take a late callout for my own business. It was dark and raining heavily. I was sitting in the middle of the left-hand turn lane in the Mary Hill Bypass. This is a small section of freeway in town with a speed limit of about sixty kilometers, but everybody flies through at about a hundred.

I had the green light for myself, but it was also for oncoming traffic. I waited my turn to dart in between vehicles to make my left-hand turn. The last car goes by, and I see a large semi-trailer truck some fifty yards away. This is more than enough time to get through the intersection and on my way; at least it is when your truck doesn't die!

As I hit the accelerator, the van just died in the middle of the intersection. I felt the immediate sense of panic as I desperately tried to restart the van. This time, it wouldn't start.

I was now the deer looking into the headlights as I witnessed the semi slam on his breaks and jam on his horn. There was nothing I could do. Fortunately for me, this guy was an experienced driver and did not have a full load at the time. I remember the back end of the trailer hopping slightly as his whole rig came to a screeching halt. With the roads being wet, he slid slightly but still kept it in control. I don't think I am exaggerating when I say he came within twenty feet of making me a statistic on the front page of the local newspaper.

With hands shaking, I started the van and reached out my window to give the truck driver a wave to say thanks. He kind of gives me one of those, "What the fuck?" gestures and I gave him a "Don't have a fuck'n clue" gesture.

Wow, talk about having the shit scared out of you. After I checked my pants for wetness, I drove into the nearest pub for a cold one. It was at that point I vowed to take the van in to be checked first thing in the morning.

As it turns out, the van had a fuel pump in it meant for a small compact car. There was no way it was able to supply enough gas on heavy demand for a vehicle of this size. I should have sued that used car shop, but there is probably some kind of small print that states it's a used vehicle, and there is no warranty. What is it with me and vans? I have almost met my death twice driving one. I tell ya, when I retire, I will definitely be driving a luxury sedan!

Within a few months, I sold that piece of shit to another plumber. Never met the guy; it was a deal through a mutual friend. I got the cash and signed the papers needed . . . done. I heard through the grapevine he was in an accident with it only a few weeks after he bought it from me. I did get the fuel pump fixed, but God only knows what else was duct taped together. I knew the sooner I got out of that rust trap, the better. Hope he wasn't hurt.

I have always kept a good credit rating, and things were going good with business. So, I leased my first brand new van, a beautiful Ford Econoline 250. It was a great service van and, I must admit, I've always loved the Ford product.

I now had a new van and was looking professional. I even had work shirts made up with my own logo that I designed. I was finally looking as good as I felt. I was starting to feel proud of myself and my accomplishments. I was now able to demand a little more on the subcontractor pay scale, as I was able to represent other companies well and look professional with a reliable vehicle.

Once again, Stan paid me the money I wanted without hesitation, but Mags had his reservations about paying more. It wasn't anything personal between us; it was just a matter of trying to decide what is fair to bill out and what isn't. Once again, I state as I write this, looking at it from the other side of the coin today, I completely understand what his side of the debate was back then.

Stan's company was really starting to take off. Although Mags and I have been friends for over thirty years, we have never really been the type to hang out with each other on weekends or after work. I really don't know why; we just never really have.

I was now starting to hang out more with Stan and his group of friends. He was beginning to hire more guys for his crew, and it was not uncommon for us to get together on the occasional Friday night for beers. He was now giving me the majority of the work, and I was making better money working for him. There was never a point where I wanted to take Mags out of the picture, but I know there were a few times where I'm sure Mags wanted to take ME out of the picture. He would phone to book me, and I would have to say "Sorry, Stan has me booked for the next three days."

He would let out a long breath and just say, "Okay, no problem. I'll just call the customer and we'll book it for later."

I could hear the frustration in his voice.

I did not want to stop the good thing I had with Stan. I soon met his family and eventually was introduced to and started dating his wife's cousin. It just seemed to fit.

It was also a different experience with the customer clientele. Stan's work was strictly through advertising, while Mags's was from past customers or a close knit group of locals. I was now experiencing a wide array of different people, all in many areas of the lower mainland and many from different walks of life.

I remember one call for a plugged toilet at a condo complex. I knocked on the door to be greeted by this rather attractive young lady, maybe in her late twenties. It was a hot summer day, and she was wearing tight jeans and what appeared to be a typical men's dress shirt, the kind you often see your favorite female movie star wearing in a typical "chick flick" as she gets out of bed in the morning to make the eggs and bacon. I said hello, and then she explained the problem.

I eventually had to remove the toilet to attempt to rid the blockage, but could not help but notice, with the occasional glance, that this attractive young lady was not wearing a bra.

To make things even better, the dress shirt was rather see-through in the light.

I soon had the toilet off the flange and had to get a hose into the unit to have any luck of dislodging the block. This meant I had to take the toilet outside onto her balcony. I asked if she had a hose hooked up, she did.

This young lady was nice enough to offer to help me as I was clearly having a bit of a struggle trying to get this crapper out of the washroom and through the back door in such tight quarters. It did not help that the hallway and surrounding area were completely cluttered. As I lay the toilet down on its back, she proceeded to grab the hose.

Now, you have to picture the situation here. This attractive young thing is now out in the sunshine, with a somewhat see-through white dress shirt. It's buttoned rather low to accommodate the hot day. She proceeds to bend over to get the hose into the precarious places of the toilet to help me out. Well, let's just say the view was spectacular.

I had to muster up all the professionalism I could, with the utmost amount of gentlemanly demeanor. But I must admit, I have never taken so long to unplug a toilet. Don't ask me what the clog was because I wasn't really paying attention to that portion of my job.

But wait, I know what every guy reading this is thinking. "Kev, you lucky bastard!"

Yes, I know, but wait. This gets even better!

My favorite beer is Guinness. I even named my black lab after the beer. For those of you who have not tried the nectar of the gods, it's a dark ale with lots of good nutrients. They actually used to serve it to the soldiers in hospital during war times; but I digress.

Anyway, during this service call, I could not help but notice that part of the clutter in the hallway was a full twenty-four pack of Guinness beer. I remember glancing at it thinking how thirsty I was, and that such a fine trophy should not be placed on the floor of a hallway.

It was at this point that the object of my attention says to me, "Do you drink beer?"

I then replied enthusiastically, "Why yes . . . yes I do, as a matter of fact!"

It was at this point she walks over to the pack of Guinness and explains that she was recently married—lucky bastard—and that they bought this beer for the wedding that nobody drank. (Heathens!) She asked if I wanted it.

Trying to hide the fact I was about to become giddy like a schoolgirl, I said, "Yes, how much would you like for it?"

She told me it was my tip for doing such a great job—I figured the dress shirt was my tip, but who am I to choose, eh?

I think I replied something cheesy like, "Well, I had a great helper."

I soon got to thinking, *Kev, she's married. Just give her the bill, take the beer, and walk away!*

I did so, and could not help but smile all the way home that day. Yes, life was good.

I recall another project where I was ripping out an old boiler system and installing a new one. The whole project was going to be about three days, and I did not have a helper. The homeowner was this crazy Portuguese lady who was a widow, maybe in her late fifties. This lady was awesome.

I say "crazy" with all due respect, because she would just say whatever was on her mind with no hesitation about what anyone else thought. And the language used . . . wow! I've heard cleaner mouths on sailors and truckers.

Over the three days, she and I became friends, and I think I heard everything there was to know about her late husband, the neighbors, and everything in-between. Along with all the problems in the world, she was always on the soapbox about something. I must admit, she was rather entertaining.

The last day I was hooking up all the electrical, which includes the thermostats around the house. As I walked through all the rooms, I could not help but notice the myriad of pictures on the wall. Here's where the story gets good.

Once again, I repeat, we live in a small world and you never know who you're going to meet from one day to the next.

I was upstairs by the fireplace in the living room. The thermostat was just off to the left, when my eye caught a picture that stopped me in my tracks.

It was a picture of an old girlfriend.

We dated for a few months when I was still early in my plumbing apprenticeship. She was an attractive girl and, despite a few years, she looked pretty much the same. It was obviously somewhat of a professional photo, as she was dressed nicely, and looking rather good, I must admit. I also couldn't help but notice a couple of things in particular were rather larger than they used to be when I dated her. I'll let you figure that one out.

So now the thought process starts to go through my mind. *Is this lady her mother that I never met? She must be some kind of relative, maybe an aunt?*

I was too curious not to ask questions, so I proceeded carefully.

"Uh, who's this beautiful lady in the picture?" I asked.

My customer looked at the picture and to my surprise, said, "That fucking bitch, do you know her?"

Wow! Holy shit! Did I just hear that? This was obviously not a daughter or a relative, so now I was really curious. I chose my reply carefully stating, "I think I might have gone to school with her at one time. How is she related to you?"

The reply was she was her daughter-in-law. Apparently she was none too happy about the marriage to her loving son. "That fucking bitch does nothing but spend his money. He buys her everything, and she's never happy. Even bought her a new set of boobs. I hate that bitch."

I chuckled to myself; good to know I never proposed to this one! Sounds like her son was the poor bastard who took over after me.

Then she asked me, "How do you know her? Did you fuck her?" Wow, this lady never ceased to shock me.

"Uh, no. No, nothing like that. I just thought I recognized her, but I must be thinking of someone else."

I decided to cut the conversation short on this one because I could see a huge can of worms in front of me, and my mouth was about to be the can opener if I continued.

But I went home that day thinking, *Wow, funny how things work out. What are the chances of doing a job for my ex-girlfriend's current mother-in-law?* Small world, indeed.

Work with Stan's company was keeping me busy and paying me well, but there was always this little voice in the back of my head that just seemed to tell me this could all come to a crashing halt at any time.

I could have easily accepted a higher-ranked position with him and become some kind of partner, but a little voice continued to remind me Mags had worked his craft slowly and built a solid clientele list. Stan was relying on massive amounts of advertising, which gives a company large overhead. This worried me and I began to ask more questions about how the business was being run, and who he was starting to employ.

He began to hire people with questionable backgrounds. One guy, who shall remain nameless, had a past history with cocaine. He was great with the gift of the gab. I must admit, he and I became friends, and I often enjoyed hanging out with him over a few drinks. But I found out through the grapevine he "allegedly" had lost all his money to cocaine addiction, and then ripped his father off of all his money to support his habit. I believe there was also a marijuana growing charge as well that somehow never stuck.

The problem is, even though this guy was "clean" and starting over, it still makes you wonder about their credibility as a person to even do those things in the first place. The scary thing was he and Stan became close, and this guy was now running the company with him.

Stan had little experience in the plumbing field, and his new partner had no experience in the plumbing and heating field whatsoever. And, these two were running the show? Yikes!

It was time to make a decision about were my loyalty was. Which side of the fence did I want to be on? The other problem was, the more I got to know Stan on a personal basis, the more frustrated I would get. I must admit, he's a very likable guy, quite personal. The issue I had with him was he loved to talk about how great he was, how much money he had made, and how much more he was going to make.

It was always a "look at me" type of conversation when you had a few drinks with him. He was the complete opposite of Mags in this respect and, speaking of respect, I started to realize I had not been showing much of that to my true friend, Mags.

It was not long after this I received a call from Mags. He was obviously not happy, and in his stern but respectful tone, he read me the riot act. He stated how he felt a little betrayed and somewhat slapped in the face, and I had to admit he was right. Stan and I were beginning to clash slightly in our opinions about work, so I decided to back off with my work for his company.

Mags and I patched up a few differences, and I apologized for not remembering where my loyalty should be. I do remember him asking some questions that came back to haunt me slightly. He asked, "What direction do you want to go? Are we still a team, or are you going off on your own?"

These were hard questions to answer, but I tried to be as honest as I could for the moment. I had a good thing with Mags, and I did not want to ruin it. I told him not to worry, I was sticking with him a hundred percent and any jobs for me would be on my own time, not his.

Work began to slow up with Stan's company, and I was receiving fewer calls from him for work. As time always tells, I had made the right decision to get back with Mags.

Sometimes you have to remember your roots and where you came from; it's not always about the money and status.

Unfortunately, Stan's company eventually became a victim of becoming too big too fast, and he folded. He went back to the grind working for others and attempted to start another company of his own, but I don't believe the thing ever really took off. I spoke to him recently, and we had a good bullshit session. I was happy to hear he was still plugging away, and that his family was well. Stan has always been one of those guys you really want to like, but something just tells you to keep your distance. Deep down, I think he's a good guy. I think he just needs to stop trying to become a millionaire over night. Slow and steady sometimes wins the race over speed and power, but what do I know? Whatever he's doing, I wish him well.

Chapter 23

Viva Las Vegas Baby. Thank You, Thank You Very Much!

I was finally starting to get my personal life back on track. I was now officially divorced, and my ex and I had finally sold our home. The rainbow to that whole rainy cloud was that we made great money on the place, and actually had a bidding war, as we sold for more money than we were advertising for.

Throughout this whole process, I had to do a lot of banking. Everything from changing accounts to opening new ones and re-positioning old ones. There was this one bank teller I had been dealing with for most, if not all, of this procedure. She and I never really had any "sparks" of interest between us on the romantic level, but she was great to talk to and always left me with a smile and a quiet confidence all was going to work out in the end. I always thought it strange that, of all the tellers, I always ended up with her. Turns out it wasn't such a coincidence, but we'll get to that later.

I now had the finances and pre-approval for a mortgage and, with luck going my way, hopefully a new home to start my life over. I now needed a real estate agent. I remembered the gorgeous blond my old buddy Dean had used to sell his home, so I looked her up and gave her a call. She remembered me and agreed to meet me for a consultation.

If I remember correctly, I put on my best clean shirt with a little cologne in hopes that this could be a new start. Nope!

As usual, the hot ones are always taken. And by a fireman, no doubt! Damn those firemen! Always saving people and keeping themselves in shape. I hate those guys! (Just kidding.)

She and I did have some good talks, and I valued her professional opinion. She fully understood where I was in life and seemed to genuinely care about what I had to say. After a few weeks of searching, I finally found a great starter place. Not too big, and a little farther out of town than I wanted, but at least it was a newer home, and it had a hot tub! Yee haw!

I was disappointed to lose my beautiful real estate lady, but I did keep in touch with her. I phoned her a couple of years back and was happy to hear she married her fireman, and they now have a child together.

It felt great to finally be doing things like cutting my own lawn again. That may sound weird to some people, but I really do enjoy shit like that. I had a bit of extra money kicking around after I settled in, so of course, buying the new big-screen TV was a must. The other thing I decided to do was jump on board with an idea me and the boys had been talking about for quite some time . . . going to Las Vegas!

This is another beautiful thing about running your own business. As long as there is a business theme or official reason of business to go on a trip, you can write it off. Sometimes, the reason or motive is a bit of a flimsy or grey area, but that's where a good accountant comes in!

I decided to see if any plumbing or heating trade shows were coming up in the Las Vegas area. It did not take me long to find something that worked for me, and I had only to call my cousin and all mutual friends.

If you have never been to Vegas, it's something you should put on your "bucket list" to do. Even if you're not a gambler or drinker, there is still so much to do in Vegas. One of the hotels even has a man-made beach and a long flowing lazy river. Jimmy Buffet has his official pub down there and Vince Neil, from Mötley Crüe, has a tattoo shop on the strip about a block down. Awesome!

My cousin Murray and I love to go to Vegas. When it comes to arranging a trip there, his rubber arm is easily twisted!

I must admit, over the years, Murray and I have tilted back many a pint and have had a plethora of good laughs. I don't have a brother, but he's probably the guy I would choose if the good Lord gave me the choice to have one. He's one of the most honest guys I know, and I'm blessed to call him my friend.

After a few phone calls and searching the Internet for good deals, we had a full crew of partiers. This trip had "drunk fest" written all over it.

It has often been said that what happens in Vegas, stays in Vegas. Well, just for you folks, I'm going to break that rule because, like a good joke, some things are just too good not to share.

As I sit at my desk writing this, I am looking at a picture of me with a couple of my buds from my cousin's crew, Bruce and Todd. We are sitting in the lounge of the Imperial Palace Hotel, enjoying a cold beer. It was taken on this trip; the date written underneath is October, 2004. We are smiling and giving the finger to the guy taking the picture.

I remember he was this loud, obnoxious guy who was pretty drunk and wanted to start a friendly conversation with us. We tried to shut him up, as we had just walked in and were tired from the flight and check-in, but you know how drunks can be!

I asked him to take our picture and he agreed. Just before the flash went off, Bruce flips out the bird. I knew exactly what he was doing, so I followed suit. After the picture, the drunk says, "What's with flipping the finger?"

I quickly replied, "Private joke for friends back home."

He took that as a reasonable answer and ordered us all a drink. That's what I love about idiots: you can make them look like idiots and they don't even know it. Then they buy you a drink on top of it. Nice!

After the divorce, buying a new home, and getting the business back on track, it was time to let lose. Bruce, Todd, Murray, myself, and about six others went for the trip.

We are a pretty close-knit group, and we all have the same sense of humor. For the most part, we all watch the same TV shows as well. This bodes well, because at any time, one of us can throw out an impression of our favorite character on a show, and we all get a laugh because we know who the character is.

At this time, there was a popular adult-style cartoon show called *South Park*. The characters were rather crude animations, and the language and plotlines were a bit over the edge, to say the least.

Shortly before we left, an episode aired with the main character sitting around a campfire singing songs. The uncle introduces his buddy, who has a voice box implanted into his throat. The uncle's friend puts his hand up to the box in the throat, and starts singing, "Koom-by-ya, my Lord, Koom-bye-ya."

Bruce is pretty good with the impressions, and he was breaking into this one all day. Todd and I split a gut every time we heard him do it.

(I am going to preempt this next part by saying I would never poke fun at anyone who has a voice box due to an illness, like throat cancer. I am merely pointing out the humor in the coincidental nature of it all. Please don't wish me eternal damnation in Hell or anything of that nature. Thank you.)

So later that evening, I'm hanging out with Bruce and Todd. We were feeling a little hungry after drinking all day. We made our way up to the food court on one of the upper floors of the hotel, decide on pizza, and sit down in one of the large booths at this little restaurant. As we were slurping back a few more pints waiting for our order, an older couple proceeds into the pizza joint and sits in the booth directly behind us.

Now, to set the scene, the three of us and this old couple are the only ones in the restaurant. Todd had an odd look on his face as he was facing the entrance. Bruce and I had our backs to the area, so could not see what the couple looked like.

Todd shakes his head and looks at us in all seriousness. He points his finger at both of us and says, "Not a word out of either of you. Not a chuckle, not even a titter."

We had no idea what he meant, so asked him, "What the hell you talking about?"

He shook his head. "You two are going to find out soon enough, so I'm just warning you now. Not a word."

For the life of us, we could not figure out what he meant, so decided to turn around to view the couple now sitting behind us. Todd sternly says, "NO!"

Soon enough, the waiter comes over to take the couple's order. The wife orders first.

Seconds after, the same voice from the *South Park* episode, in that raspy, computer monotone, says, "Mmm, I'll have the house special. Mm, extra cheese. Mmm, small . . . mmm . . . with a Coke."

Bruce and I realized what Todd had been warning us about as we looked at each other. We wanted to remain respectful to this gentleman's misfortune so did not want to break out into laughter. After all, he would have no idea why we thought this was funny. It was all Bruce and I could do to contain ourselves. I had to laugh so hard I thought my feet were going to explode!

Todd sees us going red in the face holding back the laughter, and he points the finger at us one more time saying, "I swear to God, I'll kick ya both under the table if you start laughing. If you start, I'm gonna start, and that makes us all look like assholes."

Bruce scrunches his face and puts his head in his hands. I look at Todd and start to make a face of pain as I hold in the giggles.

Then, the other finger points at us. "I'll do it. I'll kick you both in the balls so many times, you'll be begging for a kick to the shins."

We managed to hold in the giggles at the risk of a kick under the table. We certainly didn't want to offend anyone, but seriously folks, what are the chances of that scenario happening at that particular time? Every time this gentleman spoke to his wife, the images of the "Koom-bye-ya" *South Park* came to mind. Bruce and I would look at each other with a smirk, only to have Todd put the finger out and say, "NO, DON'T EVEN THINK ABOUT IT!"

I enjoy playing Black Jack and sometimes three-card poker, and recall the next day of the trip I was not doing well at either. My cousin enjoys playing the slot machines, so I figured it would be an ample opportunity for me to hang out with him, have a couple of free cocktails—free when you gamble—and try my luck.

There is a very popular slot machine that takes its theme from the big TV show *Wheel of Fortune*. My cousin and I usually try our luck at that one, but only play the twenty-five cent machine. This time, Murray decides to go big time, and puts a hundred bucks in a one dollar machine. It takes three credits to give you a shot at spinning the Wheel of Fortune, so at three dollars a pull, it adds up pretty quick.

I watched him go through one hundred dollars in no time, without even a sniff. I felt kind of bad for him, and he was obviously pissed off. Sometimes those machines are pretty "tight."

I was then able to envision what was going to happen. Someone else was going to sit down, put in a few bucks, and then bam! They were going to get the payout because, sooner than later, this machine had to spit back some big money. I figured, who better than me to be that person.

I waited until I knew he was finished with the machine, then I told him my thought process on the payout. He agreed, told me to sit down, and give it my best shot. I did so, and put in a hundred dollars of my own.

I distinctly remember telling him in jest, "Don't worry, Mur. I'm gonna win the big money and get you your hundred back!"

I think we both knew that was the beer talking, and neither of us took it seriously. Murray walked away to another area of the casino. I guess he either didn't want to see me lose either, or couldn't bear to see me win after he had his ass kicked.

I bet three credits a pull and sure enough, by the fourth pull, I had the chance to spin the big Wheel of Fortune. The money increments, just like the show, range from twenty-five to a thousand dollars. When playing a dollar a credit, these numbers would represent actual money winnings.

I spun the wheel and drooled in anticipation. I expected to maybe get a hundred or so, but as God is my witness . . . Bam. Ding. Ding. Ding. I hit a thousand dollars!

My jaw dropped and I didn't know what to do. I wanted to high-five somebody but nobody I knew was around. I calmed myself down, and grabbed my payout ticket from the machine. I went directly to the cashier booth, where they gave me ten crisp, brand new, one hundred dollar bills. Wow! That was nice!

When I went to tell my cousin, I remember acting like a giddy schoolgirl. I was so excited. I was talking faster than an auctioneer on cocaine. It must have looked like I had to pee as I was kind of doing this odd dance only white guys can accomplish. Then I did something he wasn't expecting. I gave him his hundred dollars back.

"What's this?" he asked.

"I told you I was going to get your money back. I'm a man of my word!"

He refused it at first, but after explaining I just won a thousand bucks, he took the money.

I have always said that good karma and positive energy always comes back to you. I hope so; if not, I'm out a hundred bucks!

Todd and Bruce have always been a couple of guys you just love to hang out with. They are both quick with the funny quips and have a great sense of humor. Both are the type of guys who really don't seem to worry about anything and are really casual and down to earth. That whole group of friends, including my cousin, is easy to hang out with because you never have to be someone you are not. You are respected for who you are, not what you bring to the table.

Todd has always had a kind of "anything goes" attitude toward life. It was our last night in Vegas, and Todd was really letting loose. He wasn't the only one, but we'll get to that. I remember it being about two in the morning, and we all had a plane to catch fairly early. I hate hangovers, especially when I have to fly, so I told the guys I was heading to bed.

I had lost track of where the rest of the group was by this time. After the first day or two, we would just text message each other as to where we were or what we were doing. Some were at the Flamingo, but Todd, Bruce, and I were sharing a room at the Imperial Palace.

Those two were still in party mode, so they gave me a "cheers" and took off to catch the nightlife. I went back up to the room, brushed my teeth, and did some basic packing to alleviate the rush in the morning.

The suite was a little cramped for three, but we didn't care. It was just a place to crash and shower before heading out for the next day.

There were only two beds. I somehow drew the short straw and got stuck with an old army cot that was pushed into the corner of the room. It wasn't bad, but it had a spring that kept sticking into my back. Todd and Bruce got the double beds— lucky bastards!

I was just getting comfortable when I heard a key open the door. Here's where the fun begins, kids!

I wear contact lenses, so I obviously did not have them in at this time. I opened my eyes to see two figures standing in the doorway laughing. One looked like Todd, but the other person was definitely not Bruce. I knew this for starters because Bruce is a white guy, and very pale at that. This person was black and of the female variety.

I put my glasses on to see what was going on. Todd looks at me with a smile and says, "Sorry to wake you, but I brought back some company."

"No problem," I said. "But it's three in the morning and we have to be at the airport in a few hours."

I got the "whatever" hand wave and soon asked where Bruce might be.

"I think he's playing the slots somewhere," was the response.

Todd was always a good talker, so I figured he met this girl and charmed her to come up to our room for shits and giggles. I could not help but notice that, not only was she unattractive, but she also had a black eye. Of all the chicks in Vegas, he picks one with a black eye. Wow!

She sits on Bruce's bed and says hello with a southern accent. She tells me her name is Desiree.

"How you boys doing tonight?" she asks.

I tell her things are fine, and we engage in small talk while Todd makes himself a drink from the vast array of booze bottles on our table. After making his drink, Todd asks her, "What can I get ya?"

She asks what we have, and Todd offers her a gin and tonic.

"I ain't never had no gin before. Is it good?" she asks.

"Ya," Todd says. "It's Tanqueray."

For those who don't drink gin, Tanqueray is a good brand, often found in a green bottle.

She agreed to have a gin and tonic and, after taking a sip, proudly stated "Mmm, I like this gin and Tanqueray!"

We looked at each other with a smile, as we did not want to correct her and make her look stupid. She obviously meant gin and tonic, but who were we to tell her what she liked. Todd and I to this day will be at a bar, and one of us orders a gin and Tanqueray, just for a laugh.

There were a few moments of awkward silence as we all kinda wondered what was going to happen next. It kinda had the feeling of a plotline from a bad porno in the seventies. I just needed my velvety robe and a bad moustache.

Desiree breaks the ice by asking, "So, what do you boys wanna do?"

Todd, now sitting on his bed, looks over to her and says, "I don't know, but I think you should start by showing us those titties."

Did I just hear that right? Did he just ask some girl he just met to show us her titties?

I looked at her, waiting to hear some comment like, "You're a pig," or something of that nature.

To my surprise, she says, "Okay," and proceeds to take off her top.

Wow! This is great. Where did Todd find this one? *Vegas chicks must be easy*, I thought.

"Ya, that's what I'm talkin' about," Todd says.

He gets off the bed and starts playing with this girl's breasts . . . I couldn't believe it! Todd looks at me as he's tuning her nipples like an old transistor radio.

"C'mon, Kev, give them a try."

I look at Desiree for some sort of approval, and she smiles at me and says, "Go ahead."

I'm thinking, *this is awesome,* then I proceeded to get up and help myself to a good ol' fashioned boob fondle. Todd starts laughing and yells out. "Atta boy, Kev!"

I gave her a little wink and waited for the next move. Todd had that under control, as he asked her, "I think you should show us that big, black booty!"

To my surprise, the pants came off to her wearing a G-string, and she started to give us a little striptease dance on the bed.

At this point, I didn't care about the black eye; I was having too much fun. It seemed too good to be true, and it soon was.

After we all sat down with a fresh drink. Todd looks at her and asks, "So, how much for me and my buddy?"

Holy Shit! She was a hooker!!

Now, the rest of you readers have probably figured this out a few minutes ago, but I'm pretty naïve to these things. I've never paid for sex in my life! Then I started thinking, *Todd actually picked an ugly woman with a black eye, and is willing to pay her for sex! Wow! He must be drunk! I'm thinking this girl should have paid US to have sex with HER!*

She looks at us both and gives us a price. I have no idea if the price meant the two of us separately, or a threesome, or whatever. I just knew you couldn't pay me to have sex with this woman.

I politely asked Todd if I could speak with him privately. I pulled him outside the door into the hallway. "Holy shit, dude. How drunk are you?"

He gave me an unconcerned look. "What?" he said.

I replied, "Dude, have you not noticed she fell out of the ugly tree and hit every branch on the way down? For Christ's sakes, man. She has a black eye!"

He laughed and said," It's late, and the pickings are slim at this hour."

I told him he's on his own and to make it quick; I wanted to get some sleep.

I went back to my cot and decided to watch some TV. There was nowhere else to go, so I thought I would just put up with Todd getting it on with Desiree, the gin queen.

Minutes later, Todd is having oral sex performed on him. It was no big deal, as we are all guys and it was kind of a "whatever" attitude. Desiree has her big butt in the air facing the doorway, and all you can see is Todd's face against the headboard with this stupid grin. It was at this point the door lock rattles, and in comes Bruce.

The first person he sees is me lying in the cot watching TV, since I'm in the corner of the room.

He asks me, "Hey, seen Todd?"

I smile and point in the direction of Todd's bed.

I'll never forget the look on Bruce's face, as the first thing he sees is this rather large black ass. He says, "Whoa! Hey! Yikes!"

Todd raises his face from the headboard, smiles, and says, "Make yourself a drink. Oh, by the way, this is Desiree."

Desiree actually stops giving Todd head to turn around and say hello. Bruce, being the ever polite gentleman, says, "Nice to meet ya, darling."

Bruce turns to me and silently mouths the words, "What the fuck?"

I looked back and shrugged my shoulders.

Not long after this encounter, Todd finally decides to take things into the privacy of the bathroom. Bruce and I can't sleep with the constant thumping on the wall, so we decide to enjoy a drink and watch the *Late Late Show*.

Not to be outdone, we soon see Todd come out to grab himself a cold beer from the mini-fridge. He's not wearing a stitch of clothing, except his top hat on his John Thomas, if you know what I mean. We both looked at him with heads shaking. He opened his beer and said, "What?"

The love session was soon over, and Todd said good-night to his black-eyed beauty. By this time, it had to be four in the morning. We all had one hell of a time getting up, but somehow made the flight. I don't think Todd was awake for much of the shuttle ride to the airport. Everyone asked why Todd was so tired. Bruce and I just smiled and asked everyone, "Have you ever tried gin and Tanqueray?"

The group of us had two different flights home. We were on an early one, and my cousin along with the rest were on a flight about an hour behind us. We agreed to all meet up for a cocktail at the Vancouver International Airport, to seal up the trip with a bang. Our group arrived, and we watched the arrivals board, waiting for the others' flight.

I stopped in the middle of my pint to say, "Hey, isn't that their flight, the one that's blinking delayed?"

We all agreed it was, and sure enough, we didn't see them for a couple of hours after they were supposed to arrive. My cousin was the first to show, but no one else was with him.

"Where's everyone else?" we asked.

My cousin proceeded with a rather scary story.

One of our good friends on the trip, Clay, has had a bad heart since he was a kid. I'm not sure how many open heart surgeries he has had, but surgeons have put a valve in his ticker to keep him going. If I have the story right, they put in a pig's valve, which closely imitates a human valve. The problem is, the life span of these valves is only about ten years and, at that point Clay has to have a new valve put in. It must be a huge procedure, but you never hear Clay complain about it.

Apparently, Clay was getting close to the end of his ten years on the valve he currently had. I think he was even scheduled for surgery later that year. He, like Todd, decided to go a little overboard on our last night in Vegas.

The last time I remember seeing him, he was almost stumbling. That was at about eight thirty, so I can imagine what shape he must have been in by late that night.

Story has it he and his wife made it to the plane that morning, but the plane was slightly delayed as they waited for the runway. Keep in mind that Clay is feeling pretty green and is most likely dehydrated from drinking the night before. The plane, waiting on the runway in late summer Vegas heat, must had been at about 110 degrees F in the seating area. There was no air conditioning in the plane, so everyone was just cooking, almost literally.

Clay's heart began to do jumps, starts, and stops. According to his wife, he went pretty pale and was almost going in and out of consciousness. When she asked Clay if she should ring the emergency button, he agreed. His wife hit the button for emergency status.

A voice comes over the loud speaker of the plane stating, "Please only press the emergency button if this is a true emergency. Please fasten your seat belts to prepare for takeoff."

As the light goes out, they press the button again. Once again, the airline repeats the message. This went on a few times until his wife finally waved a flight attendant to come over.

Clay was in bad shape. They halted the flight and went back to the Las Vegas airport where an ambulance was waiting.

Clay was suffering from dehydration and a severe hangover. They kept him in a local care unit for observation overnight. The flight was delayed a total of two hours.

Clay made it home safely the next day. Vegas almost claimed another victim.

Clay and his wife, Jody, are doing well with their three kids. They still love Vegas and even gave one of the girls the middle name of Presley. I don't see Clay much, usually twice a year at the hockey pools. He always has a laugh and a smile to give you. A great guy that just loves to party, and Vegas is certainly the place for that.

Our group of friends has made the Vegas trip almost a yearly event. Most of us have been down for the last three years in a row. We have had my fortieth birthday down there, and last year, good friends Vic and Sarah got married at Mandalay Bay. We are planning a trip this year as well. In the immortal words of Elvis, "Viva Las Vegas!"

Chapter 24

Starting Over

After recovering from Vegas, I decided to get back to focusing on work. I also decided to focus on the things in life I had always wanted to do. For many years, I had felt many of my decisions were based on what others wanted, or thought I should do. This would point directly to my parents and my peers. But now, I was back in my own house, living my life without anyone to tell me what to do.

I bought a home gym and started to get back in shape. I figured if I was to meet wife number two, I better get a move on and start looking good. I had so many things I wanted to accomplish in my life, but with a bad marriage, it just weighed me down.

My cousin Murray is an amazing guitarist. This guy knows theory and chord progressions to the point where he could teach a college class. He has hacked around in a few bands but never made it big. I remember being in my late teens/early twenties and thinking he was the coolest guy around. He had the long hair and dressed in the coolest rock fashions. Even my girlfriend at the time used to say to me, "Your cousin's a babe."

Ya, that's what every guy wants to hear, that your girlfriend secretly wants to sleep with your cousin. Great!

I had always had the goal of one day playing in a band with him. I played a little guitar myself, but was nowhere near his talent level. The great thing about playing guitar is if you know the theory behind it, you can also play the bass guitar. After all, the bass is simply the first four strings of a guitar.

Murray and Todd had been jamming on songs for a while at this point, and were starting to record some of their stuff. It sounded great. I never knew Todd had such a great voice. He is also a pretty good song writer. They had put some tracks down in a low-budget studio, but wanted to do more.

Todd is a drywaller and framer by trade, so he began to build a soundproof studio in his mom's garage. It turned out great.

It was at about this time I met their drummer. He was a guy that Todd played slow-pitch with in a beer league. His name was Vic. He was a perfect fit for the group, as he had the same sense of humor and was a real genuine guy. I would have to say he gives Bruce a run for his money as being the king of comedy. I am very proud to say he has turned into one of my closest friends.

I used to hang out with the guys on Friday nights, listening to some of their new tracks. They were still looking for a bass player, and one night Murray asked me if I wanted to fill in on the bass.

I had just enough liquid courage in me to give it a try without worrying about embarrassing myself. Murray told me what notes he wanted to fit into the song, and away we went.

I started showing interest in learning new songs. The guys still had an ad in the local paper for a bass player, and I completely understood they wanted someone with more experience and talent. But, eventually, my enthusiasms won out, and I got the gig as the bass player full time.

I played it casual, but I was thrilled to be part of the group. We jammed every Friday night, and it was always a good laugh. We would start off at the local pub after work for a few beers, with a burger and fries. Then, we would grab a bottle, and play the night away. The band room was completely soundproof, so we often went to two or three in the morning.

Murray wanted to start getting serious about things, so we booked some time at a professional studio. We practiced hard two nights a week. I must admit it was hard for me, because I lived an hour away from the jam space and had to work full time as well. We chipped in our money for the best recording time we could get and soon had a demo disc of five songs. We did enter one song in a radio contest, but did not win.

We have a mutual friend, Ian, who was playing the local circuit at the time. He got us in as an opening act to his band at a New Year's concert at a club in downtown Vancouver. It was a real dive but we didn't care. It is a total adrenaline rush to be playing onstage in front of a crowd. Something I'll never forget.

Unfortunately, life catches up with you, and the band eventually split. Everyone had greater priorities and was growing in different ways. I have a DVD of our concert and a CD of our studio stuff. I have our promo picture on my wall in the theater room downstairs. I think deep down the four of us are all proud of what we did; I know I am. When the guys come over to my place, we usually end up pretty smashed by the end of the night. Somehow, we always end up watching our concert on the big screen, and reminiscing of the fun we had.

We all became closer friends as a part of it. In fact, while writing this book, the four of us have recently returned from a fishing trip in the Interior of B.C. I can't remember ever laughing that much on a vacation.

I mentioned before I had a plethora of banking procedures to do, as I was getting separated, divorced, and then buying a new house. I had been dealing with a teller at my local bank who had kind of become a friend outside of work. We would always chat while I was doing my banking, and she would always ask how things were going with my divorce/separation. I would keep her informed with the latest news and findings of how the divorce laws work. She was married, so I really didn't pursue things in any way as far as more than a friend. She knew I was now living on my own and back on the dating scene. I asked her one day if she knew any single ladies who might be interested. She said she did, and a few weeks later, I was on a date with one of her girlfriends.

"I really think you two will hit it off," she told me. Aren't those always the famous last words?

I remember meeting this blind date for the first time. Now, I like girls with a bit of meat on their bones. Not fat, just with a few curves and bumps where women should have curves and bumps. This woman was a little on the thin side and could have used a few cheeseburgers. The other big drawback was we met at a pub, and she doesn't drink.

I was wondering what the proper protocol is for beverage consumption when at a pub with someone who does not drink. Do you drink in front of them, or play it polite and just have a soda?

I decided I was not interested in dating this woman in the least, so when the waitress came along and asked what I wanted to order, I said, "Vodka and Seven, make it a double."

She was actually very nice and at about twenty minutes into the conversation, I just looked at her and said "There's no chemistry here, is there?"

She agreed, and we were both now able to relax and just talk about life for the rest of the evening.

The next time I saw my teller, she asked how the date was. My first words were, "What were you thinking?" I explained she was not my type, and that my quest must continue.

As I recall, it was about that time when my teller and I got a little more personal. The bank was not busy at the time, so we had a few minutes to talk. She dropped quite the bomb when she proceeded to tell me she had paid special attention to my situation and was rather inspired. She had watched me go from the lowest of lows, to now fully enjoying my life and starting down the road to accomplishing many of the goals I had always wanted to do.

She leaned in, made sure no one was within earshot, and told me she was leaving her husband.

Wow! That was a bit of a shocker. Apparently, she had been pretty much a doormat for the last ten years and really didn't have much of a life. Her son was the world to her, but she was stuck at home all the time and had no social life with her husband. They were basically two people living separately, but living under the same roof.

Her reason for telling me was mainly because she was also looking to do an out-of-court settlement, as I had done.

You can get a home divorce kit, just as you would do your own will . . . or taxes. I knew all the proceedings, and what needs to be signed where, so she asked for my help. I gladly gave her my number to call, if and when she needed advice. I explained it's a big decision, one that should not be taken lightly. But in the end, if it's what you really want, it's worth it.

For the next few weeks, she called me at home occasionally, and I gave her all the advice and support I could. We were slowly building a friendship and trust in each other, without either of us realizing it.

She admitted she noticed me every time I came into the bank and hurried her customers to get me when it was my turn at the front of the line. It was the first time I started to consider if there was any possibility of a relationship with this woman.

She soon had all her ducks in a row and was planning to be out of the house by the start of the New Year. She mentioned the only issue she had was finding a place to live for her and her young son. I told her I would keep my ears open.

That evening, I got off the phone and took a good look at my current situation. I had a three-bedroom home of about two thousand square feet. I was only using one bedroom, and the other two were my office and a TV room. I sure could use help on the mortgage and really had more space than I needed. I had talked to a single buddy of mine a few weeks back about him moving in, but the two of us were not exactly compatible as roommates.

The more I started to think about it, the more it made sense to, at least, extend the offer to my favorite bank teller to see if she was interested in renting a couple of rooms.

The next time I spoke with her, she mentioned she may be moving in with her sister. I replied, "Sounds great, but you know if things fall through, I have two bedrooms here to accommodate you and your son, if you need a temporary place to stay."

I was serious in the offer, and she was appreciative.

Well, it turns out as things got closer to the end of the year, her plans to move in to her sister's place were not panning out.

She asked if the offer still stood, and I said yes. We made an appointment for her to come by and take a look at the rooms.

I remember being a little nervous when she came over; there was this strange feeling of talking with her without the buffer of a desk or telephone in front of us. She did not bring her son, but we had a good chat and she asked what I would be looking for money wise, and how the situation would work. Was she confined to her room like an overseas border? Or was she allowed to use the house like a real roommate?

She caught me off guard because, to be honest, I hadn't really thought the situation out. I told her if she was serious to call me and I would give her more details. Seems like a dumb thing to say, but at the time, I had never been in this situation before and did not know how to handle this.

She phoned a couple of days later saying she was serious. By this time, I had worked out the details and it was settled. I was to have a new roommate on January 1, 2005.

The agreement reached with her ex was they would each have their son for a week at a time. He's a great kid. Pretty easy to talk to, and we both love to play video games. Needless to say, we hit it off almost immediately.

Because the agreement was shared cohabitation, it was a bit of an adjustment for me. It was good in the sense that it made me remember to pick up dirty laundry, and to make sure I was courteous in doing things, like wiping down the counters and cleaning my dishes.

I'm happy to say this beautiful woman's name is Wendy, and last year I officially made her my wife.

She never moved out, so I guess it wasn't that temporary of a move. She was, and is, the most caring woman I have ever been with. It's a great feeling when you find someone who is not only a best friend, but knows you better than you know yourself at times.

I watched how she proceeded through her divorce, and noticed she was never harsh, always fair to the situation, and put her son first. She would always take the time to do little things for me, because she knew I was busy with work.

I would come home on a Friday from work, there would be a cold beer waiting for me in the fridge with a little smiley face sticker that said, "Drink me."

To this day, she still puts little love notes in my lunch she religiously packs for me. I've probably gained ten pounds since then, but at least I'm never hungry!

After going through the bad times of my divorce, I almost had a bitter taste in my mouth about relationships. I remember saying I would never marry again. But, never say never. I now could not picture my life without my Wendy. She is without a doubt, my best friend, and I look forward to telling her about my plans and my dreams every day when I come home.

Chapter 25

Breaking Off On My Own

So, at this point in our story, my personal life was back on track and all was great. My work with Mags was quite steady, but I was also able to handle my own customer calls in-between. There was a good balance between us, and neither was complaining.

Because I was now in a relationship, it was easier to hang out with other couples. We began to spend more time with Mags and his wife Paula, as the four of us got along quite well.

After a few drinks on the patio one night, Mags tells us of his plan to get a bunch of people together for a vacation. He's always been a fan of Mexico, so we decided on the Mayan Riviera.

You have to know my buddy Mags. He's not the kind to go fishing and enjoy the peace and serenity of a lake. No, not Mags. He's the type of guy who often says, "Penguin, if we're going fishing, there better be a five hundred horsepower motor on the back of that boat. I wanna see whale tails spraying out the back, the music pumping, and bikini babes serving cocktails! Yup, that's my buddy.

So, we plan this trip to Mexico. There will be about eight of us in total. Mags is always the guy who researches these trips, and finds the best deals and accommodations. Then, when he gets there, he makes friends with everybody he meets. Honestly, within a couple of days on a one-week vacation, he knows the manager by name, the bartenders by name, the maids by name ... and the crazy thing is, they know him by name. He'll get their email addresses and keep in touch with them.

Honestly, he's a blast to hang out with, just a personality magnet.

The trip was still months away and everything was great, except for one nagging bug that kept chirping in my ear. I had made a good reputation for myself in the local area for a plumbing/heating technician who was reliable and priced fairly. I was beginning to get more and more calls for work on my own. It was getting to the point where I could pretty much survive on my own customer base. But, what about my deal with Mags? What was I to do?

I mentioned in an earlier chapter about the fact it's not all about money and prestige; always think about a solid future. But, was continuing with Mags my future?

I was now fully set up with all licenses and insurance to fully and legally run my business. I would make about twenty dollars an hour more doing work for myself instead of working for Mags. I could not help but hear the ringing of the words when Mags asked me, "So, what about your own business? When will you take off to start that?"

I remembered telling him I was happy with our situation and wasn't going anywhere, and that was genuinely true . . . for the time frame when I said it.

I think it's inevitable that every child eventually has to get up, spread its wings, and leave the nest. My time was getting near, if not already here.

In asking a lot of other tradesmen about what to do, they all said the economy is at an all time high, and this is the time to get out and make the money. I was also getting burnt out doing the jobs for myself after hours from Mags or on weekends. I was also tired of losing calls because I was committed to jobs with Mags.

I decided to start looking at the numbers. I would add up all the calls I had to turn away, all the money I made or could have made with my own calls, and see if it was feasible to make it solely on my own. Now that Wendy had moved in and was helping out with finances, my overhead was lower. This meant I wouldn't have as much pressure or worries about steady work. As long as I watched my pennies, it wouldn't matter if I only did twenty hours a week. I would be earning far more money per hour working for myself.

After many hours of looking at stats and thinking about the repercussions and ramifications of my decision, I decided it was time to go solely on my own. But, the next decision was how to go about this gently.

Of all the changes in my life and decisions to follow through on, this was one of the hardest. I always feel comfortable talking to my dad when it comes to decisions like this; he always has my best interest at heart, and it comes with that old school thinking when times were a little simpler. He reminded me this is what I had been working toward and had wanted for a long time. Do not miss the opportunity and leave yourself asking "what if?"

I asked him what an accepted time frame would be to give to Mags before I changed things. He said, in his day, the general rule of thumb when leaving a job was to give two week's notice. So, this is what I decided to do.

To explain the situation with more detail, I was not looking at completely walking away from all work involving Mags. I actually wanted to continue working with him, but just on a different pay scale and on my terms.

You see, when starting out, I was not able to sustain myself strictly relying on my own customers; I had to be a subcontractor and survive on work given to me by other companies. But now I had enough customers of my own that I no longer needed to accept jobs at a lower rate of pay.

The amount of business coming in gave me the power to refuse customers and contractors not willing to pay full rate. I knew the phone would soon ring with someone who would pay the asking price. To put it plain and simple, I would no longer be working for Mags and fitting jobs in for myself; I would now be working for myself and fitting jobs in for Mags.

In the past, all materials sold when working for another company would have profits going into their pockets. I would now be selling my own parts and supplies, thus allowing me extra profit on the markup.

It was a bold move, but it was time. I needed to make the change, not only for the money, but also to be taken seriously as a man who was standing in the shadow of no one.

I had a feeling this was not going to go well. Mags was the one who had introduced me to a wealth of good contacts and people in the industry. He was always the guy that stuck with me when times were tough, and I was maybe leaning a little hard on him for more pay. He was a personal friend to me when I went through a tough divorce, and to top it all off, I did, and still do, respect the man immensely.

But the bottom line question still remained. Did that mean that this working agreement would stay as is until the end? I don't think so. A change had to eventually come, and when would the right time be? The time was now and I had to do it.

I knew I would be a bumbling mess if I tried to do it over the phone, so I did it via email. The tough thing about email is you don't get to hear the person's tone of voice or inflection of expression. This sometimes makes things sound colder and much more heartless than you want. I can only imagine how the message must have come across.

It was about the middle of the month, so if I gave the start of the next month for the implementation date of my new charge rates, I figured that would be a fair two weeks, as my dad had mentioned.

I worded it as professionally as I could, explaining that as of the first of the month, I would be solely on my own. My rates were listed very clearly, and if he wished to use my services at these competitive rates, I would be more than happy to continue doing business with him.

It might have seemed slightly cocky, but I was just being professional. As soon as I hit "send," it felt like I had lit a fuse and was waiting for the bomb to go off.

On a personal level, Mags would often send me funny jokes and videos via email. I did not receive a call that night or the next day. I expected some kind of response but got nothing. I was able to figure out he was pissed at me, because I no longer received any of the funny emails. Word started to spread at the local wholesalers we both dealt with. I began to hear things like, "So, I heard you ripped Mags off and screwed his company."

Things were starting to get blown out of proportion. I don't think anything was said by Mags himself, but these things have a way of getting around a small group.

I honestly don't remember what the first contact was after that. I don't remember if I couldn't stand the tension and called him or vice-versa. I do remember us eventually having a long talk about it, and his biggest issue was I did not give ample time with my decision to leave. He felt a couple of months were more appropriate than a couple of weeks.

I won't bore you with every detail of "yes, I did" and "no, you didn't," but suffice to say, he was pretty pissed at me.

But, we have known each other for over thirty years and were getting closer as friends than we had ever been. This was really killing me inside. It was great to now be on my own, but I felt like I had lost a best friend to do it. Was it worth it?

The worst part was knowing we had a Mexico vacation coming up that was supposed to be full of mirth, merriment, and fun! Was the trip still on, or would he actually pull out of going?

I kept my mind busy with work, and fortunately, it was looking more and more like I had made the right decision for my business. I was bringing in more money than I ever had. My customer base was growing, and Wendy and I were a happy couple. We were even talking about maybe moving into a bigger place. But the fruits of my labor seemed dampened by the fact that one of my best friends thought I was an asshole.

But, time has a way of healing many things. It slowly started to appear that Mags was seeing my side of things, understanding my decision to leave was nothing personal. I was relieved when he called one night to discuss the Mexico trip.

It was only a month away at this point, and I was looking forward to going. We spoke very matter-of-factly, almost like it was a business meeting between the presidents of two countries avoiding war. We agreed we would enjoy ourselves and not talk business on the trip. I agreed, but deep down I hoped we would soon be the friends who used to play ball hockey together in the back alley as kids. You can never replace memories like that.

Chapter 26

Señor Penguin and the Mags . . . In Mexico!

Our "business trip" was about to begin. I remember arriving in Mexico, and the first thing you smell when getting off the plane is that humidity in the air. Man, was it hot! Once we arrived at our resort and got our rooms, it was happy hour. I'm not sure what the first "cheers" was celebrating, the fact we were in a tropical paradise or the fact we survived the drive from the airport. Holy shit!

If you ever take a cab in Mexico, first do some research on how many pesos it should cost you. They know you're a tourist and will quite often try and overcharge you. These cabbies make piss all for wages and do what they can to survive. Mags had all this stuff researched before we got there. He is awesome to go on a trip with. The other piece of advice is buckle up! These guys are driving the Corona 500 out there on the streets. They're crazy!

We had a great dinner and a few drinks, and packed it in fairly early from a long day of flying and getting up early for the airport. But, the next day was party time!

We hung out around the swim-up bar most of the day. The weather was great and, because it's all inclusive, the drinks are free. Yup, as many as you can shove into your drunken yap! I love Mexico! The laughs were flowing as much as the beer was, and my buddy Mags was in prime shape.

Now, you have to understand Mags and his wife are like Barbie and Ken. Mags is a good-looking, well-built guy, and his wife is a combination of Shania Twain and Eva Longoria.

The two of them have great personalities to go with the great looks, so people just tend to gravitate to them. Well, the next thing you know, Mags is chatting up this couple from Boston. Apparently, his family owns a funeral business, and she was a stay-at-home mom; but let me tell ya, most moms don't look like her. Wow!

Their names were Sean and Stacey, and they were an interesting couple, to say the least.

Mags and I were having so much fun I think he forgot he was supposed to be pissed off with me. The subject would get touched on every now and then, but the wives would change the subject and remind us this was a "fun only" business trip.

After God knows how many drinks at the swim-up bar, it was time to shower up and get dressed up for a nice dinner. We were all pretty much looped by late afternoon, and when the drinks are free, you just keep going.

As we all know, booze tends to bring up emotions, and something had to give between me and Mags.

We phoned their hotel room to see if they were ready.

"C'mon down, you guys; let's have a cocktail before dinner," Paula said on the house phone.

I was barely seeing straight, but it sounded like a good idea. We arrive to find Mags putting gel in his hair and dancing to his favorite Nickleback song—"Photograph," I think it was. The only problem was, he was doing so in his underwear.

"For the love of Christ, dude, put some clothes on," I told him.

"Why, Penguin? I'm gonna rock out with my cock out, hang out with my wang out!"

Wendy and I burst out laughing as his wife just shakes her head.

"That's it. I'm heading to a different resort," was my reply.

The big meathead eventually got dressed and the ladies went into the powder room to do . . . whatever it is you women do. This gave Mags and me a chance to talk and, after that many drinks, the whole business situation came out in full force!

I think the ladies thought we were going to get into some kind of fight, but we just needed to clear the air. The great thing about it was there was no disrespect, calling each other names, or throwing insults. It was mainly a clearing of the air and listening to both sides of the coin. He felt very disrespected by what I had done, and I explained being my own man was something I had worked hard at achieving for years.

It took us a while to talk it out and, I must admit, by the end of it, we both had tears in our eyes. We are both pretty confident in our masculinity. Good thing, because we gave each other a big hug and I said, "I love ya, buddy."

He replied with. "Love ya, too, Penguin."

I paused as I looked at him and said, "I'm glad you're finally wearing pants when you're telling me that."

We all had a good laugh and enjoyed the rest of the evening. I felt the weight of the world come off my shoulders.

I mentioned meeting the couple from Boston earlier that day at the swim-up bar, Stacey and Sean. We met up with them at the lobby bar after dinner and got to know them better. Sean starts telling us all the crazy shit that happens when you run a funeral home.

He recalls this one time when it was a hot Friday afternoon and the funerals were running a little behind schedule that day. The guys working the backhoe and the front loader to dig the dirt for the graves get paid by the hour and, just like the rest of us, want to get off work and have a few cold ones as soon as the day is over.

I guess this one day they are doing a burial where the casket is to be lowered into the earth at the end of the sermon. If all goes well, the priest should say his "ashes to ashes, dust to dust" by about four thirty and the boys would get on the machinery just before five to put the casket in the ground. The family throws the roses in the hole, and that's the ceremony . . . if all is on schedule.

Well, as Sean tells it, these two guys are young bucks and didn't really care the funeral was running late. Their concern was getting a few cold ones and heading out to see the Bruins game. Time was of the essence, so they did what they had to do to hurry the process along.

It was nearing five and the priest was still yapping. These two guys look at their watches, look at each other, and decide to start lowering the casket into the ground . . . while the priest is still giving the speech! Sean's killing himself laughing as he's watching from afar. The casket's being dropped in the earth, and the priest is frantically turning pages from the Bible. He's talking faster and faster, and the poor family is looking at each other in amazement, as they are not quite sure what to do. The front loader guy is starting to dump earth back in to cover the casket, and the family is tossing roses in frantically . . . what a gong show. But, they get paid by the hour and when your time's up, your time's up—pardon the pun.

Sean's wife Stacey was a nice looking lady, and she hit it off with everyone. I could tell she and Mags were getting along quite well, and this was not just because of her bubbly personality. Mags loves the ladies with the fake boobs and, believe me, Stacey had quite the rack on her. We headed to the resort's nightclub later that night. Our other friends on the trip had joined us by this time, so it was quite the party atmosphere.

It didn't take long for Wendy and me to feel the effects of being in the sun all day, not to mention we were just plain tired and boozed out. We opted to get to bed at a reasonable time—two in the morning—while the others got up to who knows what.

Next morning, Wendy and I are showered and were ready to meet the crew at our designated meeting point, the breakfast buffet at nine. We had no idea how late they'd been out but were glad to see them arrive. They all looked a bit tired but shook off the hangover and joined us. I get chatting with Mags after breakfast and asked him how the rest of the evening went. He proceeded to tell me the group went back to Russ and Aaron's suite for a few drinks after the club. (These were two single guys in the group) Mags then told me to grab a couple of beverages, as he had some pictures to show me. Boy, did he ever.

He pulls out the digital camera, and aside from the typical pictures of everybody making stupid faces and drunk poses, there comes these pictures of Stacey sitting on a hanging chair in the balcony of the suite. The pics started with a couple of sexy poses, then a multitude of shots with her top off, showing this beautiful set of big boobs!

"Holy shit, dude. How did you pull those off?" I asked.

He proceeded to tell me she started talking about how she always wanted to be a porn star, and I guess Mags asked her to show the merchandise.

"Where was your wife at this time?" I asked

"She was with me."

"Where was Sean?" I asked.

"He was in the other room when I took them. She asked his permission and he said 'Whatever.'"

Wow, these people from Boston are really easy going. The pictures were passed around the group for a bit of a chuckle, but we are all adults and chalked it up to a good time.

Later that afternoon, we are all at the swim-up bar again—weird, I know. Sean and Stacey came up to say hello, and we started the party all over again. I remember asking Stacey if I missed anything good after I went to bed. She just rolled her eyes and said she had a little too much to drink.

We agreed to meet them at the lobby bar after dinner again, and by this time, I think half the resort had seen Stacey's rack via Mag's camera. We had got to know the bartenders quite well, so Mags decided to show them. The bartenders remembered her from the night before and passed the camera around, giggling like school kids who had never seen a set of boobs. This is where the story gets even better.

A half hour goes by, and sure enough, in walks Sean and Stacey. The bartenders must have planned this, because they get a few shooters lined up for Stacey and she willingly drops them back. The bartenders waited a few minutes for the alcohol to do its magic, and then proceeded to all line up at the front of the bar. The one guy yells something to her in Spanish. Once they have her attention, they all lift up their dress shirts, exposing their bare chests. We all knew about the pictures by this time, so had a good laugh at what they were imitating.

Stacey stands up and says proudly in her Boston accent," You guys wanna see my boobs?"

The bartenders all start clapping, hollering, and whistling. They grab a bottle of tequila from behind the bar, and start chanting something in Spanish.

Stacey looks over at Sean, who isn't even paying attention. "Hey, Sean. Can I show these guys my boobs?" she yells across the bar.

Sean looks at her from across the bar and says, "No, honey!"

Stacey looks as disappointed as we all did. She says again, "C'mon, honey, these guys really want to see my boobs!"

Let me tell ya, they weren't the only ones.

Sean looks at her and says, "Ya, whatever!"

Keep in mind, the bar was about twenty-five percent full. There weren't any young kids around, of course, but there was a decent crowd in there besides us.

She looks at the bartenders and says, "Are you guys ready?"

Next thing you know, the top is up and she is displaying these breasts as proudly as a kid winning a prize at the local fair.

The funniest thing is, Mags comes running out of nowhere and, without hesitation, starts taking pictures. I still have the picture somewhere, and what's priceless is you can see Mag's wife laughing her ass off in the background. She's a pretty good sport.

The bartenders, along with the rest of the lounge, start to clap. Hilarious! You can't make this shit up, folks. I swear to God, it happened.

That night, we didn't go too crazy as we had planned a trip for the next morning. We would depart at nine in the morning to Tuloom, the ancient city of the Mayan people. What amazes me is that these pyramids and dwellings were built thousands of years ago and are still standing. This is the twenty-first century and we can't get shit to stand more than a few hundred years. Go figure.

Wendy and I decided it would be a good idea to get some kind of breakfast before we go. We had no idea how much we would be walking, or how long it would be until our next meal. This was about seven in the morning, so we decided on room service.

When looking at the menu, you have to pick something simple so as not to be disappointed. I can assume bacon and eggs are not going to taste the same way they do here in Canada, so I went with the simple basic cheeseburger and fries.

When it arrived, I was watching some very attractive local newsgirl talk about the weather in Spanish. I didn't really care what she was saying, if you know what I mean. I was not paying attention to the fact my burger patty was not cooked very well; in fact, it was pretty much red in the middle. Wendy points this out to me and warns me not to eat it. But hey, I'm the man with the iron guts. I can eat anything, or so I thought. I told her it would be fine, but after eating, I thought to myself, *This isn't AAA Canadian beef; this is Mexican road kill from God knows what back road.* I began to get a worried feeling.

We met up with Mags and Paula and hopped on the tour bus. We once again were experiencing the Corona 500 on the roads of Mexico. Scary shit, folks! We made it safely, and no sooner did we get there and I had to use the washroom, as things began to feel like they were rock'n and roll'n in my guts. I just knew I shouldn't have eaten that burger!

I entered the ugliest, smelliest, filthiest excuse for a washroom I had ever seen. It was brutal, but when you have to go, you have to go. I don't even remember what I used for toilet paper, but thinking about it now, don't know if I want to remember. I proceeded on the trip and I will make this statement that will probably hold true for the rest of my life. I have NEVER experienced heat like I did in the village of Tuloom. It must have been close to 110 degrees F. People were planning their route to see the ruins by going from shaded area to the next shaded area. There is no breeze present at the site because you are at the top of a cusp behind a cliff wall; the heat is unbearable.

We soon got out of there and went to a water theme park known as Xel-ha (pronounced shell-ha). It was a great place. We proceeded to rent snorkel gear and travelled in inner-tubes down the lazy river. It was about this time the raw burger was starting to kick in. I felt awful, and that's not a word of a lie. My stomach began to cramp up and I felt like shit. I went as pale as a ghost and wanted to pass out from the heat. I began to get the shits and did everything I could to hold back from puking. But what was I to do? Our bus didn't come for another two hours, so I was stuck there.

I excused myself and sat at a nearby picnic table in the shade. I told the others to come by and get me on their way out. Wendy gave me a big straw hat, and I did the best I could to rough it out. I eventually made it back and spent the rest of the evening having a romantic candlelight dinner with my friend, the toilet.

I hate Mexico.

After a full pack of Imodium and a good night's sleep, I was ready to party the next day. Sean and Stacey were on their way back to Boston, so we had to meet new party people. Of course, Mags never disappoints, and we soon met Nick and Dom. Wouldn't you know it, a couple of Italian guys.

They were with their wives and the ladies hit it off as usual. I felt out of place at first, as Nick, Dom, and Mags started comparing notes as to what part of Italy their parents were from. We were in the pool, so I took it upon myself to go to the swim-up bar—weird—and get us all some drinks. Mags hadn't introduced me at that point, so upon my return with drinks, he introduces me to these guys.

"Hey, Dom, Nick. This is my friend, the Penguin."

Dom looks at me and says, "The penguin? What, you know this mange-cake?"

I would normally take offense to this, because calling a non-Italian a "mange-cake" is a bit of a derogatory slang. But we laughed it off, and as I got to know them, they were pretty good guys.

Nick was your typical Italian guy that every high school had in the early eighties. He had the gold chains, the mullet hair cut, and I'm sure he had a full bottle of Polo cologne somewhere in his luggage. But, man, he was pretty funny. They were from New York. Incidentally, I was surprised to find out how many Americans don't have a clue where Vancouver is. I got everything from near Toronto to just outside of Detroit. A few were close when they said, "You guys are just north of Seattle, right?

I remember one afternoon the eight of us went shopping with the wives at this little shopping plaza just outside of the main resort. There were still a few areas in the construction phase, but one would assume the washrooms would not be one of them. Unfortunately for Nick, he found out the hard way.

He told us he had to use the facilities, and then we didn't see him for quite some time. When he eventually made it back, somebody asked him, "What the hell took ya so long?"

The story was priceless. He looks at me and Mags, and says to us in his New York accent, "You guys are plumbers, aren't ya?"

We nodded.

"Then tell me something, you wouldn't put a toilet into working order unless it had a seat on it, right?"

We agreed.

"Well," he said, "some fuck'n mook decided he would put the toilet seat on the crapper at a later date."

Mags and I were trying to be serious as we started to crack a smile at his obvious misfortune.

"I get into the can with one waiting in the chamber. I'm letting off on the breaks, and as I go to sit down on what I thought was a seat, my ass falls into the water."

Nick was a little on the heavy side, to put it politely. The girls, including his wife, started breaking into heavy laughter.

"What da fuck you guys laughin' at?"

He continues. "I couldn't stop in mid-flow, so I drop the bombs. It took me twenty minutes to dry off my ass."

At this, Mags and I broke into laughter. You had to be there to hear that story in a half Italian, half New York accent. Funny stuff, good times.

Like everything good in life, it all comes to an end. We caught the plane a few days later and came home with some great memories, pictures, and a few bottles of tequila. I think Mags and I have told the story of Stacey's boobs and of Nick's "letting off on the breaks" at every party. We still laugh to this day.

Chapter 27

What's Next?

As I look back at all I have done to get to this point, it really doesn't seem that long ago. I remember being a kid, hearing all the adults say, "Don't be in a hurry to grow up. As you get older, the years just fly by." Man, is that true.

I have worked hard to establish a pretty solid group of regular customers in my business, and these people keep things going when times are slow. If I have learned anything over the years, it is definitely this: It's not the job that's difficult; it's dealing with the people.

Some people are great and completely understand you're just human. Some even give you a tip. Others think because you're charging a good buck, you better be the second coming of Christ and perform a miracle. Then on top of it, they are late paying their bill. Nothing pisses me off more than a customer calling to say he has no heat and desperately needs me to come out. You could tell him to call someone else, but you don't. You go out because they need you. But, when it comes time for you to get paid, they conveniently forget how badly they needed you and take their sweet ass time in writing that check.

Sometimes you have to fight traffic tie ups or construction problems on the highway. I wish people would be a little more forgiving when I'm a little late. I do the best I can to get there by leaving myself a reasonable amount of time for the drive.

I remember last year when I arrived at my first call of the day about twenty minutes late due to traffic. As he opens the door to great me, I give him a pleasant, "Good morning."

This asshole proceeds to give me a dirty look, and then begins to tap repeatedly on his watch, obviously letting me know I'm tardy. I was in no mood for any bullshit after dealing with lower mainland rush hour, so I picked up my tool bucket and proceeded to walk back to the truck.

Now, I realize this sounds a little cocky, but I knew in the dead of winter, most companies are booked solid, and you waited at least three days to get someone out. I also knew he had no heat, and his wife and kids would be pissed at him if it wasn't fixed. I knew, as well, my phone would probably ring in the next hour for another job, one with a customer that would probably greet me with a much more courteous demeanor.

As I walked away, he apologized up and down for his actions and explained he had to get to work. Every minute I was late meant another minute he didn't get paid. I thought about it from his perspective and understood where he was coming from. But, I then explained I wasn't late because I slept in; it wasn't my fault. We both agreed a phone call would have smoothed the situation and, at that, I went about finishing the task at hand.

I try to be open-minded with people, and for the most part, a little patience goes a long way. You never know what battle a customer has been fighting to put them in a shitty mood.

I was recently in a home where an older gentleman was in rough shape due to his multiple cancer operations. He was a really nice guy, and I felt bad for him as he told me what a great soccer player and golfer he had been back in the day.

I hated to see good people get taken advantage of, and this was definitely the case. There are quite a few large companies out there that, perhaps, are just victims of hiring bad employees, but they work on commission sales. The more shit they sell you, the more money they make. The customer gets duped into buying shit they really don't need.

This older gentlemen was the neighbor of a good customer of mine. She introduced him to me, because he had spent ridiculous amounts of money on an old, inefficient furnace, and it still wasn't working. I explained how a new energy-efficient furnace would pay for itself in a few years. He agreed, and I installed one.

He then had an old gas fireplace with a big crack down the middle of the glass. This is a carbon monoxide leak potential, so rather than waste money trying to track down parts, we installed a new one much more efficient on fuel.

As I arrived to start the job that morning, he had all his food items out of the fridge and freezer. Everything was thawing out or going rotten. He asked if I had done anything to the electrical system. I hadn't. When I checked the fridge, the compressor was shot. I ran home for him, and grabbed my largest cooler and filled it full of ice. Between me and the neighbor, we were able to save most of his food until the repair guy could fix it the next day.

I tell this story not to look like a hero; I think anyone with a heart would have helped this guy. I tell it because there are not many companies left that go the extra mile to make a difference. I like to think it's little things like this that have kept people calling me back.

I couldn't bear to see this poor guy have any more bad luck, or any other companies try and cheat him by overcharging and not doing quality work. But sure enough, the streak was not over.

I had to get into his crawl space to run a gas line for his new fireplace. As I entered the area, the sight was all I could bear. It was COMPLETELY filled with dead rats and rat feces, everywhere. I told him to get a cleanup crew that dealt with this sort of thing, as I was not going down until it was done. He agreed, and I made it very clear the whole crawl space was infested, and he should make sure the company he hired got all of it before he paid them.

I returned a couple of days later to finish the job, and I almost could have bet the farm on how the cleaning job went. Sure enough, they bet on the fact this elderly gentleman would not be able to get in there to check for himself. He was charged over three hundred dollars, and they cleaned an area of about ten square feet. I told him to cancel his check immediately. He got them on the phone and I gave them shit. They were back out the next day to do it right.

I don't understand how these companies are still in business. Treat people the way you want to be treated; it's that simple.

I recently had another situation—quite similar, only it was rather comical. This old couple was from India, I believe, and obviously had some health issues. I'm sure the place had not been cleaned in about twenty years. The tub was full of green algae with pasty soap scum, and the carpet had not seen a vacuum in as many years either. The couple's son was living there, but he looked pretty useless. As I fixed the leaky pipe, the wife came up to me with the vacuum cleaner head and says to me, "You fix? You fix?"

"Uh, no, ma'am. I don't fix vacuums."

She shoved the head back at me a second time and says, "You fix?"

The next thing you know, I've got the vacuum apart and found the belt that turns the head was missing. I stretched out an old O-ring to fix it.

As I wrote up the bill, she dropped parts of a broken screen door in my lap. "You fix?" she says.

"Uh, I really have to get going ma'am."

"You fix? You fix?"

I was soon taking apart the screen door compression arm, and eventually had it all fixed. The topper was when she walked down the stairs with a bucket and sponge and said, "Windows . . . you clean? Yes?"

I flat out explained, "No, I do not clean windows."

She then says, "Not today . . . maybe next time . . . yes?"

I just nodded my head and said, "Maybe next time."

It never ceases to amaze me the amount of people that live like pigs. I'm not talking about elderly people that can't physically do the work; I'm talking about healthy people who have no excuse to live that way. I don't care how you live your life, but when I have to put my health at risk to work on a bacteria-infested floor of urine and fecal matter, it now affects my well being and my health. I'm not talking a little dust here, folks. I'm talking caked feces and urine stains around the toilet when I come to work on it. C'mon, use your common sense. Some people just don't get it. I had to stop work at one customer's place because I was that close to puking with all the pubic hair and piss rings on the floor around the toilet. If you're having a plumber over to do work in the washroom, for the love of God, please use bleach and give it a good scrub. Thanks!

Speaking of toilets, the whole idea for writing this book started with a joke to many of my customer's saying I would one day write a book called *101 Things I Pulled Out of a Toilet.* It always amazes me how things get down there in the first place.

I've pulled out pagers, cell phones, electric razors, all types of figurines, hair clips, hair brushes, broken bottles, pens, pencils, large erasers, nail polish bottles, and the one that always stands out was a pair of Armani designer frame glasses.

No one at the business knew what was clogging the toilet. When I pulled them out, I got to thinking, *Who the hell loses a pair of seven hundred dollar glasses down a toilet and doesn't tell anybody?*

The moral of this next story would have to be things are not always as they appear.

My dad and I were installing a hot water tank at a customer's home in my local area. While we were doing that, the customer had a young kid in the backyard digging trenches to put in drain pipe and drainage rock. The kid looked about sixteen and was busting his ass working in the summer heat. He looked as if he hadn't packed a lunch or had any water with him.

My dad and I stopped for lunch, and I asked if he was hungry. The poor kid looked like he hadn't eaten in days. He admitted he was, so also threw him a cold, bottled water. He thanked me and stopped to take a break. He asked about the plumbing trade, as he was a hardworking kid looking for a direction to go. He reminded me of myself years ago. I told him it was a good trade to get into, and wished him good luck as we all got back to work.

At the end of the day, I'm giving my customer the bill for the tank install. The young kid was finished his work and asked to borrow my customer's phone. I heard him in the background talking to someone I assumed was his mom or dad. He was complaining he was a long way from the leisure center and asked if he could be picked up closer to the customer's house. I could hear his dismay and disappointment in the answer. He sauntered out the front door and I got to thinking, *The leisure center . . . that's about twenty blocks away.* Not a distance anyone would want to travel after a hard day digging in the sun.

I billed the customer, and my dad and I started heading back to my place for a cold beer. As I was driving home, I came upon the young kid at the job site. I decided to do this kid a favor and give him a ride to his destination.

"Hey!" I said." Need a ride to the leisure center?"

He recognized my van. "Ah, dude, that would be sweet!" he said.

I explained we only had two seats in the front of the van, and they were occupied by my dad and me. The only place to sit, if he wanted a ride, was on the old tank in the back of the van. He said that was fine. He opened the back door of the van and hopped in. I drove off and thought nothing of it.

Forward to about a week later. I am doing a job for a good customer that happened to be a cop. I was there for most of the day. He arrived home to ask how I was doing and the rest of the pleasantries. He paid me for a job well done, and then asked if I wanted a beer. As we're sitting back on his deck he said to me, "I'm going to mention this because you should be a little more aware of your surroundings when you do things."

I felt slightly concerned at his tone. He proceeded to tell me last week his son witnessed my van picking up a young kid outside of the local high school. He watched the kid get into the back of my van, and then I drove away.

I never stopped to look at the area I had pulled over in to give the kid a ride. Now that I think about it, it must have looked a little weird.

Because it looked rather suspicious, the son remembered my license plate number and told his dad. Yikes! Fortunately for me, this guy knew me pretty well, and he assured his kid it was not as it appeared. I explained the situation and we had a good laugh about it.

My cop buddy warned me my van is a travelling billboard, and you always have to be aware what you do because your business name and number are plastered in big, red letters. I had never really stopped to think about that, but I do now. I always think twice before I'm about to give someone the horn or the finger on the road.

Just my luck, you try and do something nice for a hardworking young kid, next thing you know, you're looking like a pedophile! I can just see it now, the local papers having a picture of my van with the headline "Local Plumber Suspected of Child Abduction." Yikes!

Speaking of having my number on my van, I recall a day when I was running late and was driving like an asshole. There was this tour bus of old people in front of me, and they were driving at a snail's pace. I was late for my call, so I passed them on a double yellow line. Not the smartest thing I have ever done, and not very safe. The bus caught up to me at the next light, and the driver takes down my number and decides to call in to tell my "office" what bad drivers they have on the road.

I guess he was under the impression we were a big company, and he was going to get a manager or phone desk clerk. He, of course, phoned me directly because I'm the only one in the company.

I answered the phone to the irate bus driver. Looking in my rear view mirror, I could see him talking. I had to think quickly, and fortunately for me, I did.

I answered with "I'm very sorry sir, did you happen to get the van's fleet number on the driver's door?"

He answered "Uh, well, no. I did not."

I calmly replied, "That's okay, sir, I think I know who the driver was, and we're looking to fire him anyway. Thanks very much for the call."

That satisfied him, and I escaped another bullet. You always have to be aware of what you do when your number is in big letters on what you drive.

The whole thing comes back to what I've been saying all along. It's a small world and you never know who you might meet. Always think twice about burning your bridges because your enemy today may be your friend tomorrow.

Speaking of never knowing who you might meet, I'm having lunch last week and this guy walked up to the van window as I'm chewing on a burger.

He proceeds to ask me questions about code restrictions concerning some big renovation. He thanks me for the advice and introduces himself as we shook hands. I was rather shocked to find he has the same last name as me!

It turned out he was my second cousin—I think. His grandfather and my grandfather were brothers. I had heard of his side of the family, but never met them. We chatted for a good half hour just talking about who was who on the family tree. I found out both my grandfather's brothers were high-ranking officers in the Russian army. Some of the Batches went to live in Washington State, while others moved up to the lower mainland to find crops and farms to work. It also turned out our real last name was not spelled or pronounced the way we currently have it. Talking to this guy, he stated it was actually spelled Patsch. My dad had said he read somewhere that my great-grandfather was a travelling judge who went by the name of Johanas Batsch. Others say our name could have been spelled Betz. Wow, Geneology.com, here I come!

Whatever my last name is, I hope I have done the family proud. I hope my parents are proud of me. I hope they now see all their patience and efforts paid off. I turned out to be an okay kid, I think, though my mom may have a different take on that one.

I'm also proud that my beautiful wife wanted to take my last name, whatever it may be. I think that's the most important one of all.

Wendy and I bought a new home a few years back. We also decided on a Lab-poodle cross puppy that, as I mentioned, we named Guinness. It's kinda cool being a part-time dad, too. Wendy's son is fifteen now, and I sometimes find myself telling customers I have a son when they ask if I have kids. Some people even say he looks a little like me. Wendy says he's definitely taking after my sense of humor. Lord help us!

I've always loved the Interior of British Columbia. I love the history and raw nature, its great fishing and the clean, crisp air. We bought a property up around the hundred-mile house area a few years ago and are in the process of building a cottage.

The plumbing industry, like all jobs, has its ups and downs. But, it's always put food on the table and a roof over my head. Come to think of it, it's allowed me a few extra pleasures in life, as well. It's given me a wealth of knowledge, good friends, and lots of great stories. I'm getting older and the memory is not what it used to be. That's why I figured I better get them down on paper before I forget them. I'm not kidding. Perhaps I have inhaled too many fumes from pipe glue and solder. Yikes!

Oh well, as long as I don't forget what's really important in life. I think the Beatles said it best with the lyric, money "can't buy you love."

I see many people with shitloads of money, but they are not happy. Money can buy you temporary happiness, but the true peace of mind comes from being able to look at the person in the mirror and be proud of the person looking back.

I also want to take a few words to thank my parents for their patience over the years. My birth sign is Taurus, and I can definitely say I can be as stubborn as a bull. My mom and dad have always been there for me, whenever I have fallen or became misguided in my adventures of life. They were strict with me, and we did not always see eye to eye, but I wouldn't change it for the world. It has made me the person I am today; the person that is proud of the guy looking back in the mirror.

My final quote is one I always remember. It just seems like a good rule of thumb to live by. I think it was Hemingway who said, "My goal is to one day be the person that my dog already thinks I am."

Cheers! And may you find your passion in life.

Kevin

Lightning Source UK Ltd.
Milton Keynes UK
UKOW04f2027221117

313187UK00001B/226/P